# German Pioneer Accounts of the Great Sioux Uprising of 1862

*The Schwandt Monument*

*The Schwandt Monument, located in Flora Township in Renville County, was dedicated August 18, 1915, in honor of the following members of the Schwandt family who were killed August 18, 1862: Johann Schwandt and his wife, Christina; their children, Frederick, age 7, and Christian, age 5; John Walz and his wife, Karolina Schwandt Walz; and the son of a neighbor, John Frass. August Schwandt, age 11, ran to the nearby brush and escaped to Fort Ridgely, while his sister, Mary, was captured, and later wrote a report of her captivity.*

# German Pioneer Accounts of the Great Sioux Uprising of 1862

Edited by

Don Heinrich Tolzmann

Little Miami Publishing Co.
*Milford, Ohio*
2002

Little Miami Publishing Co.
P.O. Box 588
Milford, Ohio 45150-0588

© 2002 by Don Heinrich Tolzmann
Cover by Print Management, Cincinnati, Ohio

All rights reserved. No part of this book may be reproduced or transmitted in any form or by any means, electronic or mechanical, including photocopying, recording or by any information storage and retrieval system without written permission from the author, except for the inclusion of brief quotations in a review.

Printed in the United States of America
Printed on acid-free paper

Library of Congress Cataloging-in-Publication Data

German pioneer accounts of the great Sioux Uprising of 1862 / edited by Don Heinrich Tolzmann.
   p. cm.
Includes bibliographical references and index.
Includes: The story of Mary Schwandt, by Mary Schwandt, originally published by Minnesota Historical Society Collections, St. Paul, in 1894; and Captured by the Indians, by Minnie Buce Carrigan, originally published in serial form in the Buffalo Lake news in 1903, then in book form in 1912.
  ISBN 0-9713657-6-8 (pbk. : alk. paper)
  1. Dakota Indians—Wars, 1862–1865. 2. Indian captivities—Minnesota. 3. Schwandt, Mary, b. 1848—Captivity. 4. Carrigan, Minnie Buce—Captivity. I. Tolzmann, Don Heinrich, 1945- II. Schwandt, Mary, b. 1848. Story of Mary Schwandt. 2002. III. Carrigan, Minnie Buce. Captured by the Indians. 2002.
  E83.86 G47 2002
  973.7—dc21                                2002007601

# Contents

| | |
|---|---|
| *Epigraph* | vii |
| *Preface* | ix |
| *Acknowledgments* | xiii |
| Introduction | 1 |
| The Story of Mary Schwandt<br>Her Captivity During the Sioux Outbreak—1862 | 9 |
| The Story of Wilhelmina Busse<br>Captured by the Indians: Reminiscences of Pioneer Life in Minnesota | 27 |
| Other Related Reminiscences | 61 |
| Editor's Conclusion | 75 |
| Notes | 79 |
| Sources | 95 |
| Index | 97 |
| About the Editor | 105 |

### ILLUSTRATIONS

Front cover illustration includes, clockwise from top left: Wilhelmina Buce Carrigan, Mary Schwandt-Schmidt, the Flora Township Monument, and Little Crow.

Back cover illustration includes the Kochendorfer Family.

| | |
|---|---|
| The Schwandt Monument | ii |
| Carl and Augusta Tolzmann | xi |
| Albert Tolzmann | xii |
| Map of the Sioux Outbreak and War in Southwestern Minnesota, 1862 | xiv |

| | |
|---|---|
| Indian Camp at Redwood (engraving) | 3 |
| The Courthouse of the Military Commission (engraving) | 5 |
| Mary Schwandt | 8 |
| Attack at New Ulm (engraving) | 14 |
| Prairie on Fire (engraving) | 14 |
| Breakfast on the Prairie (engraving) | 20 |
| Camp Release (engraving) | 21 |
| August Schwandt | 23 |
| Article regarding Schwandt Memorial Dedication | 25 |
| Wilhelmina Buce Carrigan | 26 |
| German Pioneers in Renville County/The Kochendorfer Family | 39 |
| Map showing Location of Buildings at the Upper Agency, 1862 | 60 |
| Map showing Vicinity of the Upper Sioux Agency, 1862 | 60 |
| Flora Township Monument | 78 |
| Don Heinrich Tolzmann next to Friedrich Hecker Monument | 105 |

# *Epigraph*

*Soon there came a time when I did not weep. I could not. The dreadful scenes I had witnessed, the sufferings that I had undergone, the almost certainty that my family had all been killed, and that I was alone in the world, and the belief that I was destined to witness other things as horrible as those I had seen, and that my career of suffering and misery had only begun, all came to my comprehension, and when I realized my utterly wretched, helpless, and hopeless situation, for I did not think I would ever be released, I became as one paralyzed and could hardly speak . . . and went about like a sleepwalker.*

—Mary Schwandt

*The first Sunday after my capture was the loneliest I have ever spent. . . . I wondered what a change a week had brought. Where were the people now who had been at our church and Sunday school last Sunday? Were they all in heaven with the wings of angels? . . . Thus my childish thoughts ran. Suddenly I thought of my father's hymn book. I found it and in turning over the leaves I came upon the old familiar hymn, "How tedious and gloomy the hours." I knew it by heart. . . . I sang the hymn about half through and then my feelings overcame me and I laid down the book and had the longest and bitterest cry since my parents had been murdered.*

—Wilhelmina Busse

# *Preface*

$I$N THE COURSE OF EDITING WORKS by German-American authors dealing with the Sioux Uprising of 1862, also known as the Dakota Conflict, or War, I came upon two personal accounts that conveyed the experience of the German pioneers during that tragic time period.[1] Both were written by German-American women whose families had lived in Renville County, Minnesota, and documented not only their own experiences, but those of their neighbors. The first is by Mary Schwandt, and originally appeared in 1894 in the *Minnesota Historical Society Collections*. The second is by Wilhelmina Busse and originally appeared in 1903 in serial form in a newspaper at Buffalo Lake, Minnesota, and then was revised and published in book form in 1912.[2]

Schwandt and Busse lived not far from each other in Renville County, which, like other counties in the area, was predominantly settled by recently-arrived German immigrant families.[3] Their accounts were complementary, as they both focus on events that took place in the same particular area. As they are relatively unknown, or at least inaccessible today, the editor prepared them for publication to add their voices to the historical record of the experience of the German pioneers of Minnesota.

My reasons for editing this work were twofold. First, my field of research is German-American studies, and I have published a number of works dealing with German-American history, literature, and culture, and have edited many original primary source materials. I was contacted in 1992 by friend and colleague Eberhard Reichmann, editor-in-chief of the publication series of the Max Kade German-American Center, Indiana University, Indianapolis, about the possibility of translating and editing a German-language work dealing with the uprising by Captain Jacob Nix, the commandant of New Ulm during the first Battle of New Ulm. A review of the literature indicated that the work, originally published in 1887, not only had never been translated, but, more often than not, was rarely cited in works dealing with the topic—which appeared to be a major gap in the historical literature because of the pivotal role that Nix had played in the defense of New Ulm. I also found that there were other works on the topic in German, or by German-American authors, that also had fallen into obscurity, or were relatively unknown, and were worthy of being edited for publication. I agreed to take on the project, which actually then became the first in a series of works dealing with the subject.[4]

The second factor motivating me to take on the initial project is that Reichmann surmised that I, as a German American from Minnesota, might have some interest in the topic. Little could he know the extent to which he was correct, as I had grown up hearing about the uprising and the experience of the pioneers in the region, and had attended pageants and programs in Renville County and New Ulm, Minnesota, with my family. I also learned German at home, and my father taught me to read *Fraktur*, the old German type, and to read German handscript. Anyone of German descent in the region is likely to have such memories as an integral part of one's family background, but in my case there were a few additional dimensions that contributed to my interest in the topic.

In 1870, my great-grandparents had moved from their farm at German Lake, near Elysian, Minnesota, to a farm in Renville County, located in Flora Township where County Road 21 today intersects with the Minnesota River bottom road. Their farm previously had belonged to the Schwandt family, and both the farm and the region were swept up in the storm of the uprising of 1862. Indeed, almost all members of the Schwandt family had been killed, and although the uprising was long since over when my great-grandparents moved there, there still were Indians in the area, and it was not long thereafter that my own grandfather, then a child, was kidnapped and held for a ransom of food. These stories are part of not only my family's history, but also that of the region itself.[5]

As I continued to edit original documents and works, I came upon references to the personal account of Mary Schwandt. Her family's farm had been acquired by my great-grandparents, and is now known as the Tolzmann farm. Moreover, I had often heard about her family's experience, and felt that this needed to be made available as a historical document. Also, I found that a member of a neighboring family, Wilhelmina Busse, had also written a more lengthy account, and having located it, I decided that both of them needed to be made available as primary source material. This brings to the reader firsthand accounts of the experiences of two per-

*Preface* / xi

sons who were there, and I felt that few are actually aware of what it must have been like, and that these experiences need to be taken into consideration as part of the historical record. This work, therefore, aims to contribute to our historical understanding of the topic by making sources available that provide access to the experience of the German pioneers, who experienced and survived the uprising.

*Carl and Augusta Tolzmann*

In 1870, the Tolzmann family moved to the farm in Renville County that had previously belonged to the Schwandt family. Prior to 1855, Carl Tolzmann served in the Prussian Army and, like many Pomeranians, decided to immigrate to America, considered by German immigrants as the "land of unlimited possibilities." He first went to Milwaukee, Wisconsin, where his uncle's family had settled. There, he joined a group of Pomeranians that included the family of his future wife, Augusta. The group then moved to Minnesota, and pioneered the German Lake settlement, near Elysian.

*Albert Tolzmann*

*After his family moved to the Renville County farm in 1870, Albert Tolzmann (1866–1937) was kidnapped and held until a ransom of food was paid.*

# Acknowledgments

THE MAPS OF MINNESOTA ARE REPRODUCED with permission of the Minnesota Historical Society from William Watts Folwell's, *A History of Minnesota*, rev. ed., (St. Paul: Minnesota Historical Society, 1956–69), and illustrates the various places referred to in the narrative accounts.

The engravings are from an article on "The Indian Massacres and War of 1862" from *Harpers Magazine*, (June 1863), which was provided by the Little Miami Publishing Co.

Pictures from Franklyn Curtiss-Wedge, ed., 2 vols. *The History of Renville County, Minnesota*, (Chicago: H. C. Cooper Jr., and Co., 1916) display a variety of scenes from Renville County, including illustrations of Mary Schwandt and Little Crow. Other pictures of pioneers of the area are from the Brown County Historical Society, New Ulm, Minnesota. Also many thanks to Darla Gebhard, research librarian, Brown County Historical Society, for all the assistance she has provided, especially in locating these historical illustrations in the files of the society. Finally, I would like to thank my father, Eckhart Tolzmann, for the many ways he has been of assistance.

From *A History of Minnesota* by William Watts Folwell

# *Introduction*

IN THE MIDST OF THE CIVIL WAR and on the brink of the Second Battle of Bull Run, which resulted in a severe defeat for the Union Army, the attention of the nation was drawn suddenly to Minnesota. "Frustrated and provoked by a series of broken promises and by reservation policies that forced cultural change, Dakota Indian warriors began killing white traders and settlers in August 1862."[1] Twenty-three southwestern counties were depopulated, as more than forty thousand people fled their homes. As many as eight hundred settlers and soldiers were killed in the course of the conflict, which, in terms of civilian casualties, has been surpassed only by the attack of September 11, 2001, (9-11) on New York City.[2]

Should an event of the same magnitude occur today, there is no question that it would become a media event of international proportions. That the uprising took place in a pre-Information Age devoid of twenty-first century technology and media coverage lessens our understanding of the severity of the tragic events of 1862, and their impact on the people of the time, but comparing them to 9-11 imparts an indication of what they must have seemed like.

Much has been written about the Sioux Uprising, also known as the Dakota Conflict, or War, and its causes, course, and conclusion.[3] Although this body of historical writing is large, the number of personal narratives is not that extensive, and those written by surviving members of the German pioneer generation even fewer. As Germans were in fact the largest ethnic element in Renville and Brown counties, their recollections are of particular value in shedding light on their experiences and perceptions.

Renville County was north of the Minnesota River and northwest of Brown County, and both were filling up with settlers, mainly German immigrants and their families, in the 1850s. West of Brown County and south of Renville County was Redwood County, where the Sioux reservation was located. It consisted of a tract north and south of the Minnesota

River, approximately ten to fifteen miles wide on both sides of the river, and 150 miles long. By 1862, the Sioux numbered approximately six thousand, and the population of Renville and Brown Counties was also about six thousand. The total population of Minnesota at the time was 175,000.[4]

The largest urban center in the region was New Ulm with a population of more than nine hundred, situated in Brown County, and there was also a military post, Fort Ridgely, nineteen miles north of New Ulm. However, the four companies of soldiers there had been ordered to join forces with the Union Army, so that the fort was staffed only by volunteer troops. Of the thirty there, the number would grow to 180 during the uprising. The fort held its ground due to these troops, as well as the cannons that were there. New Ulm also held its ground due to the defense that was mounted during both battles. However, those in the surrounding countryside basically were on their own, and the best places to get to were either the fort or New Ulm, and, of course, as fast as humanly possible.

The impact of the uprising is clearly evident in county histories. In the two-volume history of Renville County (1916), one-fourth of the work is devoted specifically to the topic, but references and passages throughout the work relate to it, clearly demonstrating that the events of 1862 played a major role in the history of the area.[5] The Brown County history (1916) consists also of two volumes, with one being a historical, the other a biographical volume. Of the former, one-third dealt with the uprising, again denoting its importance to the area and its impact on the lives of the residents.[6]

Both authors of the following accounts lived with their families in Flora Township of Renville County, of which the county history reports that it is bounded on the north by Emmet Township, on the east by Henryville and Beaver Falls townships, on the southwest by the Minnesota River, and on the west by Sacred Heart Township. Across the river is Redwood County. Flora Township was part of the reservation until 1858, when a treaty was reached whereby the Sioux gave up the ten-mile strip of land north of the Minnesota River, and retained their holdings to the south of the Minnesota River. The "north ten-mile strip," as it was called, had not been occupied to any considerable extent, and the Indian villages and nearly all of their teepees were located on the southern half of the reservation, with the exception of Big Stone Lake. After the 1858 treaty, the river bottomland, located on the north side, was settled. When the uprising broke out, this region of Renville County would become one of the prime targets of the Sioux, and all were "pushed off by a great wave of blood and fire."[7]

*Indian Camp at Redwood*

The landscape of the township reflected that of Renville County as a whole: "The soil is black sandy loam with clay subsoil and is very fertile. The northern portion consists of rolling prairie, while the southern portion consists of the beautiful Minnesota valley and a range of hills or bluffs extending back of the river from one-fourth of a mile to one mile in width. The river and creeks are bounded by natural forests. At present (1916), there are no villages in the township. The settlements are composed almost entirely of Germans."[8]

There are several facts to be kept in mind when reading and evaluating the narratives in this volume. First, these are accounts written by survivors, who had witnessed the slaughter of their friends, family, and other settlers, and their reports not only document their experience, but reflect their antipathies and hostilities toward the perpetrators involved in these particular acts. Second, their accounts should be viewed as historical documents, which allow us to see how they viewed, perceived, and understood the events of 1862, since their stories are integral to the totality of the primary sources that need to be considered. Finally, their reports provide frank and graphic descriptions, but nonetheless they are attempts to provide factual descriptions of what happened.

In dealing with this kind of documentation, I have followed the principles used in a volume of Dakota narratives, which notes that language that could be considered offensive has not been altered, and that "such terms as used by narrators or translators remain unchanged in the narratives. The effort has been to leave narratives largely as they were originally produced, without alterations to context, interpretations, or idiosyncrasies."[9] In short, this is a documentary collection, and the narratives need to be contextualized, and viewed for what they are, namely eyewitness reports written by two women who, as children of German pioneers, had witnessed the events they describe. As such they are part and parcel of the history and heritage of the German pioneers of Minnesota, and basic and integral to the story of 1862.

## Satterlee's Summary

[*Note:* To place the narratives in historical context, the following summary of the uprising and its aftermath, published by Marion P. Satterlee in 1927, is provided. From his brief abstract, the causes and course of the events are readily apparent, as well as how precarious the situation was when a single incident set the outbreak into motion, and then spiraled out of control, leading to the wanton acts of violence and destruction that followed.][10]

The Treaty of 1851 was presented to Congress by the Commissioners, but that body made an act of its taking all Dakota lands in Minnesota, allowing ten cents an acre for a part, largely payable in annuities. Of the initial payment the Lower Indians received nothing; the $70,000 was all taken by the traders—virtually stolen. A good share of the annuities were paid in salaries to white employees, and in merchandise furnished by white contractors. This was simply political graft. In 1857 a renegade band committed the Spirit Lake massacre, and the Indian Bureau held back the annuity in an attempt to compel the peaceable portion to capture these murderers, which proceeding was morally and legally outrageous, and was deeply resented.[11] Further causes of discontent and enmity were the marriage of Dakota women by white men who deserted them, throwing families on the bands for support; abuses of Indian credit by traders, and the general destruction of Indian customs and habits.

*The Courthouse of the Military Commission*

The winter of 1861 was a bad one, and there was much suffering and hunger. The payment of 1862 was delayed till the outbreak started. Agent Galbraith, after promising to distribute the merchandise held for issue at the payment, neglected to do so.[12] These grievances and others caused a violent agitation. At the annuity payments the traders "sat at the pay table" and took from any Indian whatever his claim, whether just or not. To prevent this a "Soldiers' Lodge" was organized and Indians were ordered not to accept credit from traders. However, the delayed payment forced them to ask [for] credit. Applying in a Council a few days before the outbreak they were told by Myrick, after a consultation of traders, that they could "Eat grass or their own dung," and the Council broke up in confusion.[13] Led by Marpia-wita (Isolated Cloud), some twenty Indians on a war party against the Chippewas, killed five people at Acton. This after a quarrel with a trader. They then returned to the reservation and told of the murders. These marauders, though disreputable, were well connected in various bands. Immediately the question of surrendering the culprits arose. This a large number refused to permit. Others remembering their ill treatment and [the] withholding [of] annuities in the Inkpaduta affair, dreaded a clash with the government.

It was decided that war must come. This band started down the reservation, arriving at Little Crow's village, where he was induced to "lead the warpath." Then, picking up the bands of Big Eagle, Red Legs, Good Thunder, and others, committed the Agency massacre.[14] Capt. Marsh with about fifty men coming to the Agency were ambushed and half of them killed. Various bands commenced to rob and murder in the settlements. Fort Ridgely was attacked on Wednesday and Friday; New Ulm [was attacked] by a small band Tuesday and in force on Saturday. The drunkenness from captured liquor and other dissension disgusted Little Crow and he left with a band for the Big Woods settlements, fighting at Acton and Hutchinson. In his absence the battle at Birch Coulee was fought on September 2. Wood Lake battle was fought on September 23.

A band of the Sissetons or Upper Indians was strenuously opposed to the outbreak, and during this battle, being joined by some of the Lower Indians, took possession of the white captives and made ready to fight the hostile faction. Little Crow was whipped in the battle and now defied, he advised flight to the western wilds and left with some 200 followers. The captives were freed, and some 400 Indians arrested and tried as follows: convicted to hang–303; to imprisonment–18; hanged–38; pardoned–1; sentence revoked–1; died–1. About one-fourth of the Rock Island prisoners died there; 177 were given the general pardon of 1866. About 1,700 were banished to the Crow Creek reservation, many of whom died from the hardships.[15]

## Chronology

17 August—Murder of five settlers at Acton, Meeker County.

18 August—Attacks launched against the Lower and Upper Sioux Agencies; Captain John Marsh and troops attacked at the Redwood ferry; and settlers attacked throughout the Minnesota River valley.

19 August—First Battle of New Ulm, with Captain Jacob Nix as Commandant; H. H. Sibley appointed to lead the volunteer troops (1,400) against the uprising.

20–21 August—First attack on Fort Ridgely; Lake Shetek, West Lake, and Big Stone Lake attacked.

22 August—Major attack launched against Fort Ridgely; General Sibley arrives at St. Peter.

23 August—Second Battle of New Ulm, with Charles E. Flandrau as Commandant.

2–4 September—Battles at Birch Coulee, Forest City, Acton, and Hutchinson.

22–23 September—General Sibley advance arrives at Wood Lake; Battle of Wood Lake, with failure of the attempted ambush by the Sioux.

24–28 September—Little Crow and other Sioux leaders withdraw and the Sioux surrender and release captives at Camp Release.

September/October—Appointment by Sibley of military commission to try the Indians who participated in the uprising.

November—Sioux from Lower Agency moved to detention camp at Fort Snelling in St. Paul.

26 December—Execution of thirty-eight Sioux participants in the uprising at Mankato based on the decision of President Lincoln, who set the official death toll at 800.

June 1863—1,700 Sioux are sent to Crow Creek, Dakota Territory; the rest of the Sioux, which had numbered 6,000, scatter to the Dakota Territory.

1863–65—General Sibley's western campaign to the Dakota Territory; various murders by Sioux in Minnesota.

1866—General pardon of 177 Sioux, including the chief witness for the prosecution, Joseph Godfrey.

*Mary Schwandt*

(FROM THE COLLECTION OF THE BROWN COUNTY HISTORICAL
SOCIETY, NEW ULM, MINNESOTA)

# The Story of Mary Schwandt
## Her Captivity During the Sioux Outbreak—1862

—by Mary Schwandt

*I* WAS BORN IN THE DISTRICT OF BRANDENBURG, near Berlin, Germany, in March 1848. My parents were John and Christina Schwandt. In 1858, when I was ten years of age, our family came to America and settled near Ripon, Wisconsin.[1] Here we lived about four years. In the early spring of 1862 we came to Minnesota and journeyed up the beautiful valley of the Minnesota River to above the mouth of Beaver Creek and above where the town of Beaver Falls now stands, and somewhere near a small stream, which I think was called Honey Creek—though it may have been known as Sacred Heart—my father took up a claim, built a house and settled.[2]

His land was, I think, all in the Minnesota bottom or valley, extending from the bluff on the north side to the river. Our family at this time consisted of my father and mother; my sister Karolina, aged nineteen, and her husband, John Waltz; myself, aged fourteen; my brothers, August, Frederick, and Christian, aged respectively ten, six, and four years, and a hired man John Fross. We all lived together. My brother-in-law, Mr. Waltz, had taken up a claim and expected to remove to it as soon as he had made certain necessary improvements. The greater part of the spring and summer was spent by the men in breaking the raw prairie and bottom lands so that the sod would be sufficiently rotted for the next season's planting.

My father brought with him from Wisconsin some good horses and wagons and several head of cattle and other stock. He also brought a sum of money, the most of which was in gold. I remember that I have seen him counting the gold, and I once testified that I thought he had at least four hundred dollars, but some of my relatives say that he had over two thousand dollars when he came to Minnesota. He had brought some money from Germany, and he added to it when in Wisconsin.

Our situation in our new home was comfortable, and my father seemed well satisfied. It was a little lonely, for our nearest white neighbors were some distance away. These were some German families, who lived to the northward of us, I believe, along the small stream which I remember was called Honey Creek. One of these families was named Lentz, or Lantz, and at this time I cannot remember the names of the others. The country was wild, though it was very beautiful. We had no schools or churches, and did not see many white people, and we children were often lonesome and longed for companions.

Just across the river, to the south of us, a few miles away, was the Indian village of the chief of Shakopee.[3] The Indians visited us almost every day, but they were not company for us. Their ways were so strange that they were disagreeable to me. They were always begging, but otherwise were well behaved. We treated them kindly, and tried the best we knew to keep their good will. I remember well the first Indians we saw in Minnesota. It was near Fort Ridgely, when we were on our wagons. My sister, Mrs. Waltz, was much frightened at them. She cried and sobbed in her terror, and even hid herself in the wagon and would not look at them, so distressed was she. I have often wondered whether she was destined to suffer at their cruel and brutal hands. In time I became accustomed to the Indians, and had no real fear of them.

About the first of August, a Mr. Le Grand David came to our house in search of a girl to go to the house of Mr. J. B. Reynolds, who lived on the south side of the river on the bluff, just above the mouth of the Redwood, and assist Mrs. Reynolds in the housework. Mr. Reynolds lived on the main road, between the lower and Yellow Medicine agencies, and kept a sort of stopping place for travelers. I was young, but rather well developed for a girl of fourteen-and-a-half years, and I could do most kinds of housework as well as many a young woman older than I, and was so lonesome that I begged my mother to let me go and take the place. She and all the rest of the family were opposed to my going, but I insisted, and at last they let me have my way. I do not think the wages I was to receive were any consideration; indeed, I do not know what they were.

Mr. David said there were two other girls at the Reynolds house, and that the family was very nice, and these inducements influenced me. So I packed a few of my things together and was soon ready. My mother and sister seemed to feel badly about my going, but I was light-hearted, and said to them: "Why it is as if I were going back to the old country, or somewhere else a long way off, that you act so, when it is not very far and I shall come back soon, and it is best for me, since I am of little help to you here." So, at last we bade one another good-bye, and I went away down the beautiful valley, never to see my good father nor my precious mother nor my lovely sister nor my two dear little brothers any more—any more in this life.

How little did I think, as I rode away from home, that I should not see it again, and that in less than a month of all that peaceful and happy household but one of its members—my dear, brave brother August—should be left to me. Many years afterward my husband and I visited the region of my former home, and I tried to locate its site. But the times had changed, and the country had changed. There were new faces, new scenes and new features, and so many of them, and such a flood of sorrowful recollections came over me, that I was bewildered, and could recognize but few of the old landmarks, and I came away unable to determine where our house stood, or even which had been my father's land.[4]

When I came to Mr. Reynolds' house I was welcomed and made at home. The inmates of the house at the time, besides Mr. Reynolds, were his wife, Mrs. Valencia Reynolds, and their two children; Mr. Davis, who was staying here temporarily; William Landmeier, a hired man; Miss Mattie Williams of Painesville, Ohio, a niece of Mr. and Mrs. Reynolds; Mary Anderson, a Swedish girl, whose father had been a blacksmith in the employ of the government at one of the agencies, and myself. In a narrative, published by Mrs. Reynolds (now dead), which I have seen, she mentions a boy that lived with them, but somehow I cannot remember him. I do not now recall anything of special importance that occurred during my stay here until the dreadful morning of the outbreak. Mr. and Mrs. Reynolds had been in charge of the government school for the Indians which had been established at Shakopee's school for the Indians, only a mile away. Travelers frequently stopped at the house, Mattie and Mary were very companionable, and I was not lonesome, and the time passed pleasantly. I was so young and girlish then that I took little notice of anything that did not concern me, but I know that there was no thought of the terrible things about to happen nor of any sort of danger.

The morning of August 18 came. It was just such a morning as is often seen here in that month. The great red sun came up in the eastern sky, tinging all the clouds with crimson, and sending long, scarlet shafts of light up the green river valley and upon the golden bluffs on either side. It was a "red morning," and, as I think of it now, the words of an old German soldier's song that I had learned in my girlhood come to my mind and fitly describe it:

> O, Morgenroth! O, Morgenroth!
> Leuchtet mir zum frühen Tod!
> (O, morning red! O, morning red!
> You shine upon my early death!)

It was Monday, and I think Mary Anderson and I were preparing for the week's washing. A wagon drove up from the west, in which were a Mr. Patoile, a trader, and another Frenchman from the Yellow Medicine agency, where Mr. Patoile's store was. They stopped for breakfast. While they were eating, a half-breed, named Antoine La Blaugh, who was living with John Mooer [most likely the German name Mohr], another half-breed, not far away, came up to the house and told Mr. Reynolds that Mr. Mooer had sent him to tell us that the Indians had broken out and had gone down to the lower agency, ten miles below, and across the river to the Beaver Creek settlements to murder all the whites! A lot of squaws and an Indian man were already at the house.

The dreadful intelligence soon reached us girls, and we at once made preparations to fly. Mr. Patoile agreed to help us. Mr. Reynolds had a horse and buggy, and he began to harness his horse, having sent La Blaugh to tell Mr. Mooer to come over. Mr. Mooer came and told Mr. Reynolds to hasten his flight, and directed him what course to take. I was much excited, and it has been so long ago that I cannot remember the incidents of this time very clearly. I remember that Mr. and Mrs. Reynolds and the two children got into the buggy, and that we three girls got into Mr. Patoile's wagon with him and Mr. Davis and followed. We did not take many things with us. In our wagon was a feather bed and at least one trunk, belonging to Miss Williams.

Mrs. Reynolds' statement says that the boy started with an ox team and was killed near Little Crow's village, but I cannot now remember about this. It is singular that I cannot well remember the Frenchman who was with Mr. Patoile, when, in my statement before the commission the following year, I gave full particulars regarding him, stating that he was on horseback, and how he was killed, etc. I cannot account for this discrepancy, except that I have often honestly and earnestly tried hard to forget all about that dreadful time, and only those recollections that I cannot put away, or that are not painful in their nature, remain in my memory. The hired man, Landmeier, would not leave with us. He went down the river by himself and reached Fort Ridgely in safety that night. Mr. and Mrs. Reynolds also reached Fort Ridgely, taking with them two children of a Mr. Nairn that they picked up on the road.

Mr. Patoile was advised by Mr. Mooer to follow close after Mr. Reynolds in the buggy and not follow the road. But Mr. Patoile thought best to keep the road until we crossed the Redwood River. He then left the road and turned up Redwood some distance, and then struck out southeast across the great wide prairie. It seems to me now that we followed some sort of road across this prairie. When we had got about eight miles from the Redwood a mounted Indian overtook us and told us to turn back and go up to Big Stone Lake, and that he would come up the next day and tell us what to do. I do not know his name, but he seemed very friendly and to mean well; yet I do not think it would have been better had we done as he directed. At any rate, Mr. Patoile refused to return, and continued on, keeping to the right or south of the lower agency.

At one time we were within two miles of the agency and could see the buildings very plainly. We now hoped that it was all a false alarm. It seemed that the agency had not been attacked, at least the buildings had not been burned, and our spirits returned somewhat. But soon after we saw a smoke in the direction of the agency, and then we were fearful and depressed again. And yet we thought we could escape if the horses could hold out, for they were getting tired, as Mr. Patoile had driven them pretty hard. We were trying to reach New Ulm, where we thought we would be entirely safe.[5]

About the middle of the afternoon some Indians appeared to the left or north of us. They were mounted and at once began shooting arrows at us. Some of the arrows came into the wagon. We succeeded in dodging them, and we girls picked them up. Miss Williams secured some and asked Mary [Anderson] and me for ours, saying she meant to take them back to Ohio and show them to her friends as mementoes of her perilous experience. (In the record of my testimony before the claims commission of 1863 I am made to say that only one Indian shot these arrows, and that he took the Frenchman's horse, but it is impossible for me to now to remember the incident in this way.) When we arrived opposite Fort Ridgely—which stood about half a mile from the north bank of the Minnesota—Mr. Patoile supposed we could not cross the river, as there was no ferry there, and we continued down on the road to New Ulm. The horses were now very tired, and we frequently got out and walked.

*Attack at New Ulm*

*Prairie on Fire*

When we were within eight miles of New Ulm and thought all serious danger was over, we met about fifty Indians coming from the direction of the town. They were mounted, and had wagons loaded with flour and all sorts of provisions and goods taken from the houses of the settlers. They were nearly naked, painted all over their bodies, and all of them seemed to be drunk, shouting and yelling and acting very riotously in every way. Two of them dashed forward to us, one on each side of the wagon, and ordered us to halt. Mr. Patoile turned the wagon to one side of the road, and all of us jumped out except him. As we leaped out Mr. Davis said "We are lost!"

The rest of the Indians came up and shot Mr. Patoile, four balls entering his body, and he fell dead from the wagon. I have a faint recollection of seeing him fall. He was a large man, as I remember him, and he fell heavily. Mr. Davis and we girls ran toward a slough where there was some high grass. The Indians began firing at us. Mr. Davis was killed. The Frenchman ran in another direction, but was shot and killed. Mary Anderson was shot in the back, the ball lodging near the surface of the groin or abdomen. Some shots passed through my dress, but I was not hit. Miss Williams, too, was unhurt. I was running as fast as I could towards the slough, when two Indians caught me, one by each of my arms, and stopped me. An Indian caught Mattie Williams and tore off part of her "shaker" bonnet. Then another came, and the two led her back to the wagon. I was led back also. Mary Anderson was probably carried back. Mattie was put in a wagon with Mary, and I was placed in one driven by the Negro Godfrey.[6]

It was nearly four o'clock, as I remember from a certain circumstance. The black wretch Godfrey had been with the Indians murdering and plundering, and about his waist were strung quite a number of watches. I learn that this old villain is now at Santee Agency, Nebraska. He gave evidence against the Indians who were hanged at Mankato, and so escaped their deserved fate. The Indians shouted and were very joyful over the great victory, and soon we were started off. The wagon with Mattie and Mary went toward the lower agency, and the one I was in went off into the prairie. I asked Godfrey what they were going to do with me, and he said he did not know.

He said they had chased Mr. and Mrs. Reynolds, and he believed they had killed them. He said: "We are going out this way to look for our women, who are here somewhere." About three miles out we came to these squaws, who were sitting behind a little mound or hill on the prairie. They set up a joyful and noisy chattering as we approached, and when we stopped they ran to the wagons and took out bread and other articles. Here we remained about an hour, and the Indians dressed their hair, fixing it up with ribbons. When we came up to these Indians I asked Godfrey the time, and looking at one of the watches, he replied, "It is four o'clock."

About five o'clock we started in the direction of the lower agency. Three hours later we arrived at the house of the chief, Wacouta, in his village, half a mile or so below the agency. Here I found Mrs. De Camp (now Mrs. Sweet), whose story was published in the *Pioneer Press* of July 15. As she has so well described the incidents of that dreadful night and the four following dreadful days, it seems unnecessary that I should repeat them; and, indeed, it is a relief to avoid the subject. Since it pleased God that we should all suffer as we did at this time, I pray [to] Him of mercy to grant that all my memories of this period of my captivity may soon and forever pass away.

At about eleven o'clock in the night I arrived at Wacouta's house. Mattie and Mary were brought in. The ball was yet in Mary's body, and Wacouta tried to take it out, but I am sure that Mrs. Sweet is mistaken when she says he succeeded. He tried to, in all kindness, but it seemed to me that he was unwilling to cause her any more pain. At any rate, he gave up the attempt, and I remember well that the brave girl then took his knife from his hand, made an incision over the lump where the ball lay, took out first the wadding, which was of green color and looked like grass, and then removed the ball. I think after this Wacouta dressed the wound she had made by applying to it some wet clothes.

On the fourth day we were taken from Wacouta's, up to Little Crow's village, two miles above the agency. Mary Anderson died at four o'clock the following morning. I can never forget the incidents of her death.[7] When we came we were given some cooked chicken. Mary ate of the meat and drank of the broth. Mattie and I were both with her, and watched her by turns. It rained hard that night, and the water ran under the teepee where we were, and Mary was wet and had no bedclothing or anything else to keep her dry and warm. When at Wacouta's she asked for a change of clothing, as her own was very bloody from her wounds. Wacouta gave her a black silk dress and a shawl, which some of his men had taken from some other white woman.

Mary was a rather large girl, and I remember that the waist of this dress was too small for her and would not meet or fasten. It was in this dress she died. She was very thirsty, and called often for water, but otherwise made no complaint and said but little. Before she died she prayed in Swedish. She had a plain gold ring on one of her fingers, and she asked us to give it to her mother, but after her death her finger was so swollen we could not remove the ring, and it was buried with her. I was awake when she died, and she passed away so gently that I did not know she was dead until Mattie began to prepare the face cloths.

She was the first person whose death I had ever witnessed. The next morning she was buried. Joseph Campbell, a half-breed prisoner, assisted us in the burial. Her poor body was wrapped in a piece of tablecloth, and the Indians carried it to the grave, which was dug near Little Crow's house. The body was afterward disinterred and reburied at the lower agency. A likeness of a young man to whom she was to have been married we kept, and it was returned to him. Her own we gave to Mrs. Reynolds.

While in Little Crow's village I saw some of my father's cattle and many of our household goods in the hands of the Indians. I now knew that my family had been plundered, and I believed murdered. I was very, very wretched, and cared not how soon I too was killed. Mrs. Huggan, the half-breed woman whose experience as a prisoner has been printed in this paper, says she remembers me at this time, and that my eyes were always red and swollen from constant weeping. I presume this is true.

But soon there came a time when I did not weep. I could not. The dreadful scenes I had witnessed, the sufferings that I had undergone, the almost certainty that my family had all been killed, and that I was alone in the world, and the belief that I was destined to witness other things as horrible as those I had seen, and that my career of suffering and misery had only begun, all came to my comprehension, and when I realized my utterly wretched, helpless, and hopeless situation, for I did not think I would ever be released, I became as one paralyzed and could hardly speak. Others of my fellow captive say they often spoke to me, but that I said but little, and went about like a sleepwalker.

I shall always remember Little Crow from an incident that happened while I was in his village. One day I was sitting quietly and shrinkingly by a tepee when he came along dressed in full chief's costume and looking very grand. Suddenly he jerked his tomahawk form his belt and sprang toward me with the weapon uplifted as if he meant to cleave my head in two. I remember, as well as if it were only an hour ago, that he glared down upon me so savagely, that I thought he really would kill me; but I looked up at him, without any fear or care about my fate, and gazed quietly into his face without so much as winking my tear-swollen eyes. He brandished his tomahawk over me a few times, then laughed, put it back in his belt and walked away, still laughing and saying something in Indian, which of course, I could not understand.

Of course he only meant to frighten me, but I do not think he was at all excusable for his conduct. He was a great chief, and some people say he had many noble traits of character, but I have another opinion of any man, savage or civilized, who will take for a subject of sport a poor, weak, defenseless, broken-hearted girl, a prisoner in his hands, who feels as if she could never smile again. A few days since I saw Little Crow's scalp among the relics of the Historical Society, and may I be forgiven for the sin of feeling a satisfaction at the sight.

But now it pleased providence to consider that my measure of suffering was nearly full. An old Indian woman called Wam-nu-ka-win (meaning a peculiarly shaped bead called barley corn, sometimes used to produce the sound in Indian rattles) took compassion on me and bought me of the Indian who claimed me, giving a pony for me. She gave me to her daughter, whose Indian name was Snana (ringing sound), but the white called her Maggie, and who was the wife of Wakin-yan Weste, or Good Thunder.[8] Maggie was one of the handsomest Indian women I ever saw, and one of the best. She had been educated and was a Christian. She could speak English fluently (but never liked to), and she could read and write. She had an Episcopal prayer book, and often read it, so that Mrs. Sweet is mistaken in her belief that Mrs. Hunter had the only prayer book in camp. Maggie and her mother were both very kind to me, and Maggie could not have treated me more tenderly if I had been her daughter.

Often she preserved me from danger, and sometimes, I think, she saved my life. Many times, when the savage and brutal Indians were threatening to kill all the prisoners, and it was feared they would, she and her mother hid me, piling blankets and buffalo robes upon me until I would be nearly smothered, and then they would tell everybody that I had left them. Late one night, when we were all asleep, Maggie in one corner of the tent, her mother in another, and I in another, some drunken young hoodlums came in. Maggie sprang up as swiftly as a tigress defending her young, and almost as fierce, and ordered them out. A hot quarrel resulted.

They seemed determined to take me away or kill me, but Maggie was just as determined to protect me. I lay in my little couch, trembling in fear and praying for help, and at last good, brave Maggie drove the villains away.

Mr. Good Thunder was not there that night, but I do not know where he was. I have not much to say about him. He often took his gun, mounted his horse, and rode away, and would be absent for some time, but I never saw him with his face painted or with a war party. He is living at Birch Coulie agency now, but Maggie is not his present wife. I learn that she is somewhere in Nebraska, but wherever you are, Maggie, I want you to know that the little captive German girl you so often befriended and shielded from harm loves you still for your kindness and care, and she prays God to bless you and reward you in this life and that to come. I was told to call Mr. Good Thunder and Maggie "father" and "mother," and I did so. It was best, for then some of the Indians seemed to think I had been adopted into the tribe. But Maggie never relaxed her watchful care over me, and forbade my going about the camp alone or hardly anywhere out of her sight.

I was with her nearly all the time after I went to live with her. She gave me squaw clothes and embroidered for me a most beautiful pair of white moccasins, and I put them on in place of the clothing I wore when I was captured. Old Wam-nu-ka was always very good to me, too. The kind old creature has been dead many years, and Heaven grant that she is in peace. For several days after I first came to live with them they were very attentive, waking me for breakfast, and bringing me soap, water, and a towel, and showing me many other considerations.

I think we remained at Little Crow's village about a week, when we moved in haste up toward Yellow Medicine about fifteen miles and encamped. The next morning there was an alarm that the white soldiers were coming. Maggie woke me, took off my squaw clothes and dressed me in my own. But the soldiers did not come, and we went on to Yellow Medicine, where we arrived about noon. On the way there was another alarm that the soldiers were coming, and there was great confusion. Some ran off into the prairie and scattered in all directions, while others pushed teams as fast as they could be driven.

Four miles from Yellow Medicine I was made to get out of the wagon and walk. From this time every day there was an alarm of some kind. One day the soldiers were said to be coming; the next day all the prisoners were to be killed, etc. On one occasion a woman was killed while trying to escape. I was again dressed in Indian garments. I was told that the Sissetons were coming down from Big Stone Lake, and there was danger of my being killed if I looked like a white girl. Maggie and her mother wanted to paint my face and put rings in my ears so that I would look more like a squaw, but I refused the proposition. I assisted my Indian "mother" with her work, carried water, baked bread—when we had any—and tried to make myself useful to her. We lived chiefly on beef and potatoes; often we had no bread.

We were encamped at Yellow Medicine at least two weeks. Then we left and went on west, making so many removals that I cannot remember them. I did not go about the camps alone, and I knew nothing of what was outside. I saw the warriors constantly going and coming, but I knew nothing of their military movements and projects. A simple little German *maedchen* of fourteen cannot be expected to understand such things. I did not hear the cannon at Wood Lake, and did not know the battle was in progress till it was all over.[9]

During my captivity I saw very many dreadful scenes and sickening sights, but I need not describe them. Once I saw a little white girl of not more than five years, whose head had been cut and gashed with knives until it was a mass of wounds. I think this child was saved, but I do not

*Breakfast on the Prairie*

know who she was. I do not remember that I talked with my fellow prisoners. I remember Mrs. Dr. Wakefield and Mrs. Adams. They were painted and decorated and dressed in full Indian costume, and seemed proud of it. They were usually in good spirits, laughing and joking, and appeared to enjoy their new life. The rest of us disliked their conduct, and would have but little to do with them.[10] Mrs. Adams was a handsome young woman, talented and educated, but she told me she saw her husband murdered, and that the Indian she was then living with had dashed our her baby's brains before her eyes. And yet she seemed perfectly happy and contented with him!

At last came Camp Release and our deliverance by the soldiers under General Sibley. That story is well known. I remember how angry the soldiers were at the Indians who surrendered there, and how eager they were to be turned loose upon the vile and bloody wretches. I testified before the military commission that tried the Indians.

*Camp Release*

Soon after I was taken below to St. Peter, where I learned the particulars of the sad fate of my family. I must be excused from giving the particulars of their atrocious murders.[11] All were murdered at our home but my brother August. His head was split with a tomahawk, and he was left senseless for dead, but he recovered consciousness, and finally, though he was but ten years of age, succeeded in escaping to Fort Ridgely. On the way he found a child, five years old, and carried it several miles, when, by the direction of a German woman he had fallen in with, he left it in a house eighteen miles from the fort. The child was recovered at Camp Release, but it was so much injured by wounds and exposure that it died soon after reaching Fort Ridgely. August is now a hardware merchant in Portland, Oregon.

Soon after arriving at St. Peter I was sent to my friends and relatives in Wisconsin, and here I met my brother August. It was a sad meeting for the two little orphans, though we were most happy in seeing each other. The next year I returned to Minnesota and testified before what was called the claims commission. The government had suspended the annuities usually paid the Sioux, and directed that the money should be paid to the people whose property had been destroyed by the Indians during the outbreak, or to their heirs.

An administrator was appointed for my father's estate, and a guardian for me and my brother. I testified to the property my father had, all of which had been taken or destroyed by the Indians; but I do not remember that my brother and I ever received but an insignificant sum, and yet I do not know why we did not. It seems that everybody else, traders and all, were paid in full. Some gold was taken from the dead body of an Indian during the war, and from the circumstances, General Sibley thought the money had been taken from my father. The amount was ninety dollars, but there was a premium on gold at that time. General Sibley purchased two fifty-dollar government bonds with the money and held them for my brother and me some years. In 1866, General Sibley gave me one of the bonds and twenty dollars in interest on it, and my receipts to him for this money are among the Sibley papers in the Historical Society. A part of the year 1863 I was with the family of my old employer, Mr. Reynolds, who then kept a hotel at St. Peter. In the fall I went to Fairwater, Wisconsin, and remained with an uncle for two years. In 1866 I married Mr. William Schmidt, then and for many years afterward one of the businessmen of St. Paul. We lived in St. Paul until 1889, when we removed to Portland, Oregon. Two months since we returned to St. Paul. We have three living children, a daughter and two sons; four children are dead.

*August Schwandt*

*August Schwandt, the brother of the author of one of the accounts, was the sole survivor of the attack on his family's farm, but always wore a hat due to the scars on his head. According to the newspaper article shown on page 25, he was "tomahawked but the blade failed to penetrate the brain altho the brain was exposed."* (FROM THE COLLECTION OF THE BROWN COUNTY HISTORICAL SOCIETY, NEW ULM, MINNESOTA)

Life is made up of shadow and shine. I sometimes think I have had more than my share of sorrow and suffering, but I bear in mind that I have seen much of the agreeable side of life, too. A third of a century almost has passed since the period of my great bereavement and of my captivity. The memory of that period, with all its hideous features, often rises before me, but I put it down.

I have called it up at this time because kind friends have assured me that my experience is a part of a leading incident in the history of Minnesota that ought to be given to the world. In the hope that what I have written may serve to inform the present and future generations what some of the pioneers of Minnesota underwent in their efforts to settle and civilize our great state, I submit my plain and imperfect story.[12]

—*Mary Schwandt-Schmidt*
St. Paul, July 26, 1894

# JOHANN SCHWANDT MONUMENT DEDICATED

### With Impressive Services Wednesday—One Surviving Member of Massacred Family Present

The exercises for the dedication of the monument erected by the State of Minnesota to commemorate the spot where John Schwandt and family were killed by the Indians in the massacre of August 8, 1862, in Flora township, Renville County, about five miles directly north of Delhi, and which marker or monument was provided for by a special appropriation of the 1915 session of the legislature were held at 3 o'clock Wednesday of this week, this date being the fifty-third anniversary of the day on which the opening of the Indian massacre occurred and the exact anniversary day of the massacre of this family.

The credit for getting this monument belongs to Senator N. J. Holmberg and Representative Chas. Neitzel, the latter having had hard work to get the house to make the appropriation although the senate freely gave it.

That the shaft could be dedicated on this the fifty-third anniversary of the massacre was possible only through the untiring efforts of Commissioner Wm. Wichman and the hustling firm of Anderson Bros. of this village, who erected the same and cut the shaft from the beautiful Morton granite. It is worthy of note in this connection also that several state officials present Wednesday commented on the beautiful stone secured and the fact that so large and fine a shaft could be secured for the State for the sum of $200 when others so secured for the State have cost so much more and especially the one at a nearby place which cost the state over $2000 and and not a great deal larger and but little if any more handsome.

By three o'clock Wednesday a good crowd had assembled from Renville, Olivia, Sacred Heart, Hector, Morton, Fairfax and Redwood Falls and Chairman Wichman then introduced Judge R. T. Daly who spoke touchingly of the purpose of the erection of the marker in commemoration of the massacre of the sturdy pioneers who had braved such dangers that this fertile section of the state might be brought to perfection and enjoyed in peace by their children. Hon. D. S. Hall then followed with appropriate remarks which should be an inspiration to the younger generation. M. J. Dowling then spoke of the very favorable conditions which surrounded the present residents of Renville county compared with those of a few years ago and advised against anyone parting with Renville lands and moving to some place less favored with nature's beauties and bounteous harvests. This was followed by Major Holcomb who gave a concise statement of the facts concerning the escape of Mary. E. Schwandt Schmidt from the Sioux Indians who had massacred the other members of her family, and of which mention was made in these columns in an earlier issue. At this time it was brought out however that one brother of Mrs. Schmidt had also escaped massacre. The little fellow then a lad of about ten years of age was tomahawked but the blade failed to penetrate the brain altho the brain was exposed. In this condition August made his way in three days with others to Fort Ridgely, and later fully recovered. He is now a resident of Vancouver, B. C. Mrs. Schmidt was so overcome with grief and gratitude toward the people who had so honored her parents on this occasion that she was unable to speak and Major Holcomb acted in her stead. But finally Mrs. Schmidt consented to appear for just a minute to personally thank those present for their attendance and for the beautiful monument presented. Senator N. J. Holmberg gave an impressive address and presented the monument to the State with remarks which left few dry eyes in his audience and should have deeply impressed all with the debt which they owe the pioneers, and also took occasion to thank Commissioner Wichman and the members of the Anderson Granite Co. for their duties so faithfully and conscientiously performed. Secretary of State Julius Schmahl then on behalf of the State accepted the monument and guaranteed its careful preservation.

The statement has been made some of the exchange newspapers that this was the last of the scenes of massacre which had not previously been marked. This dedication service brought out proof of the error of this contention. For while it is true that Mr. Gilfillan has marked many of the scenes of the massacre there are still several which have not been so marked, and in proof of this Henry Schmidt of Redwood Falls, who at the time of the outbreak was a soldier and part of the time stationed at Fort Ridgely and with a company who marched to other places at the time of the massacres, spoke in defense of the other unmarked locations. His brother was - among the number of the unmarked victims, and it was also brought out that there are other families, among them that of the Kochendorfers who lived then in a house on the rise of ground near the scene of the Schwandt massacre.

Only four actual survivors of the massacre were present Wednesday, and they were Mrs. Mary E. Schmidt of St. Paul, Henry Wichman of Montana, Wm. Wichman of Morton and Herman Schmahl of Redwood Falls, the latter having been born at Fort Ridgely.

The busy harvest season and the fact that the monument was not finished until Tuesday of this week thus giving Mr. Schmahl little time to arrange a program and advertise the event doubtless accounts for there not being an even larger attendance at the dedication, but certainly nature had provide for the erection of this marker for at the site selected and near where the former Schwandt house stood, is a large boulder which made an excellent base for the shaft and right on the public road, and made an excellent place for this handsome 11 foot Granite marker to be placed.

*Article from unknown newspaper regarding the Schwandt memorial dedication. Date unknown.* (FROM THE COLLECTION OF THE BROWN COUNTY HISTORICAL SOCIETY, NEW ULM, MINNESOTA)

*Wilhelmina Buce Carrigan*

(FROM THE COLLECTION OF THE BROWN COUNTY HISTORICAL SOCIETY, NEW ULM, MINNESOTA)

# The Story of Wilhelmina Busse Captured by the Indians: Reminiscences of Pioneer Life in Minnesota

—by Minnie Buce Carrigan

## Preface

DURING THE MONTH OF JANUARY, 1903, this story was published in serial form in *The Buffalo Lake News*. From the demand made for copies of *The News*, containing the story, and from the suggestions of several of my friends, I have been actuated to publish it in book form. It is needless to say that I claim no literary merit for the book. I have simply related the facts as they occurred to me, without attempting to add thereto any polish or embellishment. I have no doubt but what the desultory manner in which it is written will be the cause of criticism, but if the little book only serves to instill in the minds of its readers a true appreciation of the pioneers of the Minnesota valley, and a like appreciation for the manifold comforts and advantages which are ours to enjoy at present, but which were not thought of by our ancestors forty years ago, then I shall feel that this story has not been written in vain.

### Forty Years Ago
From *The Buffalo Lake News*

The story relating to the capture by the Indians of Mrs. Minnie Buce Carrigan, of Buffalo Lake, has been perused with great interest by hundreds of *News* readers throughout this section of the country. The pioneers of the Minnesota valley and the survivors of those dark days of '62, when morning dawned upon a torn and dismembered community and the ruins of once happy homes, have found in this story something which recalled many incidents of sweetest and saddest memory and that caused them to live over again those turbulent times.

The experience of Mrs. Carrigan has been the experience of hundreds of others, whom ambition drove from their homes in the East to brave the dangers of frontier life amid the savage scenes of the West. Fortified by an indomitable courage and preserving energy, they shrank not from the dangers and hardships of pioneer life, but resolutely set to work to build homes for themselves and their children in what is now the rich and beautiful county of Renville.

Living at peace with the world and enjoying a certain measure of contentment they little dreamed that the peaceful community in which they resided was soon to become the theater in which was staged one of the greatest tragedies the nation has ever seen.[1] Forty years ago this county, now peopled with happy and prosperous farmers and dotted with thriving villages, was the hunting ground of the Indian and the home of the buffalo and deer. The settlement of the country by the whites was regarded from an Indian standpoint as an encroachment upon their rights, and acting upon the theory that the nation was weak because of the Civil War, the Indians determined to reclaim their land by murdering the whites.[2] A compact was formed between the Sioux and Chippewas, and those two tribes, the ancient enemies of each other, smoked the pipe of peace as they prepared for the outbreak which proved to be their Waterloo. In the loss of life and sacrifice of property no Indian conflict in the country has equaled this massacre. The burning, pillaging, murdering, and torturing that went on are awful to contemplate. One writer alludes to it thusly:

> An all-seeing eye looking down from above could have seen this avalanche of 30,000 human beings of all ages and in all conditions, their rear ranks maimed and bleeding, and faint from starvation and loss of blood, continually falling into the hands of inhuman savages keen and fierce upon the trail of the white man. And angels from the realm of peace, touched by human woe over such a scene, might have shed tears of blood, and passing the empyreal sphere one might there behold the Creator lament and draw a cloud of mourning round His throne.

## CHAPTER 1

In 1858 my parents, Gottfried and Wilhelmina Buce [Buse/Busse] with three children, August, Wilhelmina (myself), and Augusta, came from Germany to America and settled at Fox Lake, Wisconsin. My sister Amelia was born here.[3]

In the spring of 1860, in company with five other families, two of whom were named Lentz and Kitzmann, we came to Minnesota.[4] I distinctly remember many incidents of this journey. We all had ox teams and some other livestock with us. All the families were devout Christian members of the Evangelical church and, I remember, we never traveled on the Sabbath. At Cannon Falls my mother fell from the wagon and a wheel passed over her foot injuring it so severely that we were compelled to stop. The other families remained with us. The men rented land and, possibly with the exception of Mr. Lentz, put in crops of corn and oats. It was too late for wheat. My sister Caroline was born during our stay here. Perhaps it was the intention of the families, at first, to remain at Cannon Falls at least a year. But in six weeks, my mother having recovered from her injuries, they decided to remove farther westward.

The previous year Mr. Mannweiler, a son-in-law of Mr. Lentz, had settled at Middle Creek in Renville County. My father and Mr. Lentz concluded to settle near him; Mr. Kitzmann decided to remain at Cannon Falls.[5] I do not know how long we were on the road from Cannon Falls to Middle Creek, but remember the evening we reached Mr. Mannweiler's where we remained two days. Then my father took the family to a Mr. Schmidt. Soon he bought the right to a claim on which some land had been broken and other improvements had been made. Mr. Schmidt and my father put up some hay for the cattle and father went to Yellow Medicine [County] to work a month and put up hay for the government cattle at the Indian agency. Mother stayed with Mrs. Schmidt during this time. When Father returned he moved his family into an old house on his claim. All the neighboring settlers turned out to help us fix up our house so that we could live in it comfortably. I think ours was one of the nine families that lived there during the winter of 1860 and '61. In the spring of '61 twenty families came in one party and joined us. Mr. Kitzmann came up from Cannon Falls and was the first settler at Sacred Heart Creek.

Our life on the frontier was peaceful and uneventful. All, or nearly all, of the families of our settlement were Germans—honest, industrious, and God-fearing people.

Early in the spring of 1861 arrangements were made to have a German minister hold monthly religious services among us. A Reverend Brill was our first minister. We had no public school, which my father often regretted. On winter evenings our parents taught us to read German and we younger children learned to read a little in Sunday school. Religious services and Sunday school were held at the houses of the settlers. The Indians from across the Minnesota River to the south of us visited us nearly every day and were always very friendly.[6] We younger children could not speak a word of English, but most of us learned a little of the Sioux language and our parents learned to speak it quite well. All the settlers were in moderate, but fairly comfortable, circumstances and though they had to undergo many discomforts and some privations, all seemed happy and contented.[7]

In the spring of '61 my father got a bad scare, but it turned out all right for us, but not so lucky for the Chippewa Indian that came near the Sioux reservation. My father wanted to buy a gun of the Indians, and every old gun they could not use they brought to him to try. They all had guns to sell. The first gun that was brought to him as an old flintlock. Father went to examine it. He was in the house. The gun accidentally discharged, and shot a hole through the roof of our house. Father was so frightened he could not speak. I can see his white face yet as the smoke cleared. A few days later another Indian came along with a gun. Father was standing under a tree in front of the house.

An Indian came with a gun and wanted father to shoot at a stick he stuck in the ground. Father picked up the gun and blazed away at it. He hit the mark all right, but the gun kicked so hard he fell flat on his back. Mother and the Indian both laughed. This made father so angry he picked up the gun and was going to strike the Indian with it. Mother grabbed his arm and told him it would cost him his life he struck the Indian. Father seemed to understand her meaning and stood the gun up against the tree and walked into the house. The Indian grinned and took his gun and walked away, and mother told father to quit his trading with the Indians.

After that, if an Indian came with a gun to sell, father would not speak to him. One day soon after father's last gun trade a strange Indian came to our house about four or five o'clock in the afternoon. He asked my mother how far it was to Sacred Heart Creek.[8] Mother held up three fingers, indicating three miles. He started on his journey. About half an hour after he had gone one of our cows that had a young calf four weeks old running with her came running up to the house without her calf and acted as though she was crazy. My father was not at home and mother told my brother to go and follow the cow, for she had gone back again, and see what had happened to her calf. My brother followed the cow. Soon after he had gone my father came home and mother told him about it. He, too, went to look for the calf. Soon they both returned bearing the dead calf home. The Indian had cut its throat and cut off one hind quarter and left the rest on the ground. Father threw the dead calf on the ground and went to work and skinned it. He remarked that the Indian was good to leave us some of it. The next morning my father came into the house and said to mother, "I am afraid I got into trouble the other day when I tried to strike that Indian with the gun. There are fifty Indians in our door yard on horseback, all in war paint." Father sat down by the table. He seemed to be unable to move.

Mother went out to see what they wanted. She soon returned laughing and told father they were not after him at all, but they were looking for the Chippewa that had killed our calf, and they wanted him to come and help them find him. They had tracked him as far as our house. Father went with them as far as where the calf was killed, and then came home. He told mother that he would sooner lose a dozen calves than to see the Sioux kill a Chippewa. In the middle of the afternoon they returned, bringing the Chippewa with them. They had overtaken him and got him alive. That suited them better, for they could torture him to death. They wanted father to come over to the killing and the feast, but he refused.

In the spring of 1862 so many people came into the country that we did not know half of our neighbors. The church society was divided into two divisions, called the Sacred Heart and Middle Creek divisions, and each had religious services twice a month, being held in dwelling houses nearest the center of the district. I remember the spring of that year that Mr. Schwandt and his family joined our colony. I saw them first at the house of Mr. Lenz.[9]

It was about at this time that the conduct of our Indian neighbors changed toward us. They became disagreeable and ill-natured. They seldom visited us and when they met us, passed by coldly and sullenly and often without speaking. On one occasion some of them camped in my father's woods and began cutting down all the young timber and leaving it on the ground. My father remonstrated with them. He told them they could have all the timber and tepee poles they wanted for actual use, but let the rest stand. When he had spoken a squaw caught up a large butcher knife and chased him away. He came to the house and told my mother of the affair, but she only laughed at him for allowing an old squaw to drive him out of his own woods.

At another time about a week before the dreadful outbreak, my brother August came home from Mr. Lenz's in great fright. He said that Mr. Lenz had caught a nice string of fish in the Minnesota river and brought them home. An Indian came into the house and demanded some of them. "Go and catch your own fish," said Mr. Lenz. The Indian flew into a rage, and, among other things, said angrily, "You talk most now but wait awhile and we will shoot you with your own gun." Mr. Lenz was the only man who owned a gun in the neighborhood and the Indians knew how defenseless we were. When my brother had related this incident, father seemed strangely affected. He was silent for a while and then remarked to August, "Well, boy, we have all to die some time, and there is but one death," and then went out.

The peaceful Sunday before the outbreak of the following day, services were held at Mr. Lettou's house, a mile-and-a-half from our place. The Sunday school was held before the preaching. Mr. Mannweiler was the superintendent.[10] As was his custom, he gave us children little blue cards on each of which a verse in scripture was printed, and then showing us some nice red cards, told us that if we would repeat from memory the verse on our card the coming Sunday, he would give us each one of them. We were all greatly pleased at this. He closed the school just as the people were assembling for church and directed the children to remain out of doors during the services, for there seemed to be a crowd coming and the house was not very large. I remember that there was so large an attendance that most of the boys and men sat outside in front of the open door. I think there were over a hundred adults and about thirty children at the church that day.

Louis Thiele and Mike Zitlaff were sitting on a wagon tongue while Thiele's child was playing in front of them.[11] Poor Mike little thought that it was his last days on earth. He was married to Mary Juni less than a year before. They were both murdered the next day. Mr. Zitlaff was a brother to Mrs. Inefeld, who was taken prisoner.[12] Mr. Thiele saved his life by jumping from his wagon and hiding in the woods. Within twenty-four hours after that meeting, not more than thirty of those present remained alive. The others, including Reverend Mr. Seder, had been murdered by the Indians.[13]

That dreadful Monday—August 18, 1862—my father was putting up hay a mile east of our house. I remember that dinner was a little late and father complained. He was in a hurry to finish his haying that he might go to work again at Yellow Medicine to put up hay for the government cattle where he could get good wages. When he had started for his work, my brother climbed on the roof to see where our cattle were. We had to keep watch of them as they ran at large on the prairie. Sometimes the Indians would stampede them and we would have to hunt for days to find them again.

When my brother came down, he told mother that he heard shooting and someone scream at Roessler's and that father was looking toward Mr. Roessler's house as far as he could see him.[14] Mother thought maybe the Indians were shooting at a mark and wanted August to go to Mr. Roessler's and borrow some sewing needles. We did all our trading at New Ulm and often had to borrow such articles. When he returned he said, "O mother, they are all asleep. Mrs. Roessler and the little boy were lying on the floor and the boy's ear was bleeding. The big boy was lying in the clay pit and was all covered with clay."

## Chapter II
### *Murder Most Foul*

My mother was standing by the table cutting a dress for my little sister when my brother returned. "O, my God," she exclaimed, "the Indians have killed them—We must fly for our lives—You children stay here and I will go and call father." But my brother and I refusing to remain in the house, were then told to hide in the cornfield on the south side where she and father would meet us. She then ran to tell father. My brother took the baby Bertha, aged three months, and I took little Caroline while Augusta, aged five years and three months, and Amelia, aged four, walked along with us.

We had hardly reached the cornfield when the Indians came whooping and yelling around the west side of the field from Mr. Boelter's.[15] We sat down and they passed us so closely that it was strange they did not see us. They rushed into our house and we went on. Looking back we saw them throwing out the featherbeds and other articles. We reached the south side of the field safely and father and mother were already there. I think we would have been safe there at least for a time, but father taking the baby from August, started out on the open prairie. Mother took Caroline from me and tried to stop father, but it was useless. The terrible circumstances must have unbalanced his mind, naturally being very nervous.

The Indians had cleared out of our houses and were returning to Mr. Boelter's. As they were passing a little corner of the timber one of them saw father and uttered a wicked piercing yell. It was but a moment when the whole band, about twenty men and some squaws, were upon us. My father began talking to the foremost Indians. My brother has told me that father asked them to take all his property but to let him and his family go. But the Indian replied in the Sioux language, *Sioux cheche* (the Sioux are bad). He then leveled his double barrel shot gun and fired both barrels at him [father]. He [father] dropped the baby—she was killed—and running a few yards down the hill, fell on his face, dead.

The same Indian then went to where my mother had sat down beside a stone with little Caroline in her lap, reloaded his gun and deliberately fired upon them both. She did not speak or utter a sound, but fell over dead. Caroline gave one little scream and a gasp or two and all was over with her. The cry rang in my ears for years afterward. My father was thirty-three and my mother thirty years of age when they were so cruelly murdered by the Indians.

How painfully distinct are all the memories of the scenes of this dreadful afternoon. While my mother was being murdered I stood about ten feet away from her paralyzed with fear and horror, unable to move. The Indian began loading his gun again and was looking significantly at me and my sister Amelia, who lay by my side. Suddenly I regained my self-control and, believing that I would be the next victim, I started up and ran wildly in an indefinite direction. Accidentally I came to where my father lay. He had on a checked shirt the back of which was covered with blood, the shot having passed clear through his body. That was the last thing I knew. The next thing I remember was an Indian holding me in his arms, looking at my face. I screamed and he put me down.

My brother then told me not to be afraid as they would not kill us but were going to take us with them. Amelia was also there but being unable to see Augusta, I asked for her. "I have not thought of her," replied August (or Charley as we called him afterwards). "The last I know of her is when she told me to wait for her, but I couldn't." We three then rose and looked about for her but could not see her. My brother asked an Indian about her but the Indian looked at him coldly and plied, *nepo*. I knew the word meant "killed" or "dead" but I was not satisfied. I wanted to see her and told the Indian so as good as I could. He took me by the hand, my brother and sister following, to where she lay. She lay on her face and, as I saw no blood upon her, I thought at first she was alive, but when I turned over her body and looked upon her little face, once so sweet and rosy, but now so pallid and ghastly in the blaze of the hot August sun, I knew the truth. I wanted to see no more but was ready to go with the Indians as they were already waiting.

We must now go back a little to where my father, mother, and sisters were murdered and learn how my brother escaped the fate of the others. The second Indian fired at him, but as he was running he missed him, the ball striking the ground right ahead of him. He fired again and missed him the second time. Then the Indian threw away his gun and ran after my brother. When he came up to him he kicked him in the side and knocked him down. He then told my brother to come with him. The Indians believe that the Great Spirit protects those at whom they shoot twice and miss. They do not shoot at them again but give them a chance to live.

Some time after our capture we went back to Mr. Boelter's place. As we turned the corner of the woods I took the least look at our home. I have never seen it since, neither do I care to see it again, although it is not many miles from our present home.

When we came to the Boelter house we found that the Indians had already murdered the most of the family. We saw three of the children lying among some logs between the house and the well. The right cheek of the oldest girl was shot away clear the bone. They had thrown some clothes over the body of the second girl. My brother went to remove them but the Indians called him back. I think they had taken the youngest child by the feet and beaten her over a log for her dress was unfastened and her back was bare and was all black and blue. The birds were singing in the trees above them and the sun shown just as bright as ever. There was not a cloud in the sky. I have often wondered how there could be so much suffering on earth on such a perfect August day.

After we saw the children the Indians took us to the house. I did not go in at first but looked at Mrs. Boelter's little flower garden. She was the only woman in the neighborhood who had tame flowers and I used to wish that I could have some of them but was afraid to ask her. Then it occurred to me that Mrs. Boelter was dead now and I could pick all the flowers I wanted. I gathered a handful and the next morning flung them back into the little flower bed. I did not want them. Mrs. Boelter was dead; if I did not see her body I was sure of it, and was taking advantage of a dead person.

How gladly she would have given me some had she known that I wanted some. I started to go into the house but my brother, who was standing at the door, stopped me. I waited a few minutes until he went away and then looked in. There lay Grandma Boelter on the floor with every joint of her body chopped to pieces. All that winter after the outbreak I would dream about her and cry in my sleep over it. She was such a nice old lady and I thought so much of her.

Michael Boelter escaped to Fort Ridgely taking with him a baby belonging to his sister-in-law, Justina Boelter, whose husband was killed. He was at his brother's place when the Indians killed his own family. Mrs. Justina Boelter hid in the Minnesota bottoms with her two children for nearly nine weeks until found by some of General Sibley's soldiers from Camp Release, but during her wandering one of her children died of starvation.[16] When found, she and her other child were nearly dead too.

After visiting the Boelter place, four of five of the squaws started with us and the plunder which they had obtained, for the Indian village south of the Minnesota River two miles south of our house. We crossed over in a canoe and reached the reservation about four o'clock. The rest of the Indians started for Mr. Lenz's place.

Mr. Lentz and his entire family were saved except his son-in-law, Mr. Mannweiler. Mrs. Mannweiler had heard in some manner that the Indians were killing everybody. She told them they must leave as quickly as possible. Her husband was loading up already and she and her sister, Augusta, went back to Mannweiler's to ride with them. Just as they were coming out of the woods, the Indian shot Mr. Mannweiler off the wagon. Augusta Lentz was a little ahead of Mrs. Mannweiler. The Indians caught her and took her prisoner. Mrs. Mannweiler ran back to her folks and ran away with them. They went through the open prairie and reached Fort Ridgely safely. I learned these particulars from a friend of the Lentz family.

## Chapter III
### In the Indian Camp

The Indians lived in bark tents where we stayed the first night. They offered us something to eat but I had no appetite. My sister was playing about the tent when I called her to me and asked her where she was when the Indians killed our mother. "Why," she answered "I was sitting a little way from her playing with my flowers. They shot and shot. Back of me all was smoky but no ball hit me." I thought at that time that it was too bad she did not realize what had happened. But since I have often been glad that she knew so little about the terrible deed. The Indians let us stay together. We slept on bunks made beside the wall on one side of the tent with buffalo robes spread over us.

The next morning when I awoke my brother was already up. We were sleeping side by side without clothes on. The Indians never undress when they go to bed. He was crying and the tears were rolling down his cheek. I could not think where we were but all at once the horrible scene of the day before came back to me. I did not blame him for crying. I cried too. If the earth would have opened then and swallowed me I would have been thankful.

My sister awoke with a scream and asked, "Where are we? August, take me back home. I want to go to my mother." This woke up the Indians and one of the squaws tried to take her but she screamed and clung to me. This was more than we could stand and we all cried out loud. An old Indian then went out and brought in an axe and told us that he would split our heads open if we did not stop crying. We tried to stop but the tears would come in spite of the axe. Just then an old Indian widow and her daughter (a girl of about seventeen years old) came in, I knew them as they used to come to our house. I jumped off the couch and ran to the young girl and put my arms around her arm and hugged her tightly. She put her other arm around my shoulders and took me out of doors. She seemed to know that I wanted protection. She did not kiss me for Indians never kiss, but I wanted to kiss her so badly. The old lady picked up my sister and put her on her back as she would her own child and brought her out. She seemed to like the Indian mama as she called her. My brother followed us, too. It seems wrong to me to call these two Indian women squaws, for they were as lady-like as any white women and I shall never forget them.

By this time breakfast was announced which consisted of beef without salt, pancake made of flour and water with saleratus stirred in them, coffee and boiled corn. As they did not use salt in anything, I called for it, *minisku yah*, in their language, but they shook their heads and replied, *waneeche* (I could not have it). We ate but little breakfast for their way of cooking did not suit us. After breakfast an Indian girl came in with Mrs. Schmidt's blue silk wedding dress on. This circumstance made me so angry that I could have torn it off from her. Another Indian girl came in with Mrs. Kochendorfer's sunbonnet on and gave it to me but I did not want it.[17] I knew that Mrs. Kochendorfer must be dead or they would not have her clothes, so I laid the bonnet down. The next girl that came along picked it up and took it along with her.

All at once we heard a commotion outside and we all rushed to the door to see what was the matter. The Indians were bringing in all the cattle of the neighborhood. The cows had not been milked the night before nor that morning and were nearly crazy. The Indians were riding behind them on their ponies flourishing their whips and yelling like so many demons. The very earth seemed to tremble as they passed. Afterwards the oxen hitched to wagons were driven up and stopped before the tents. "These," said my brother, "are our oxen hitched to Mr. Roessler's wagon." They were too lazy to unload our load of hay and put the box on. Our black ox, Billy, was harnessed to a buggy and Billy seemed to feel proud of the distinction given him. He was owned by the widow and her daughter who adopted my sister while she was prisoner. The Indians then went to packing up their goods and loading them on the wagons.

We children were watching them when all of a sudden somebody stepped behind me and threw a blanket over my head and picked me up and ran with me to a wagon, put me onto it and held me fast. I kicked and screamed but they would not let me go. The wagon was in motion for about an hour before they took off the blanket and then I looked in all directions but could see nothing of my brother and sister and I did not see

*German Pioneers in Renville County*

When the Kochendorfer family was attacked, Johann Kochendorfer was shot down in the dooryard, and the baby, Sara, and the wife, Catherine, killed in the farmhouse. Fortunately, the father lived long enough to direct his children to hide in the brush, and they escaped to the fort, aided by Michael Boelter and the Ernest Lenz family. From left to right: Catherine, holding Margaret; John; Johann holding Kate; and Rose. The daughter, Sara, was not born when this picture was taken. The Kochendorfers were neighbors to the Schwandt family.
(FROM THE COLLECTION OF THE BROWN COUNTY HISTORICAL SOCIETY, NEW ULM, MINNESOTA)

them again for over a week. My brother said he was served the same way. All that day we traveled. The prisoners had to go bare headed in the hot August sun.

At noon we stopped about an hour. A squaw told me to sit under the wagon and she threw a blanket over my head and made me sit there. Just before we started again she brought me some meat and potato to eat. I never saw any bread from the time I left home until I got among white people again. The squaw told me (evidently to keep me from running away) that they would shoot me if I took the blanket off my head. We traveled southwest all the rest of the day. I do not know how far we went nor when we stopped as I think I was asleep for I remember nothing about it.

The party of Indians that I was with left the main force—about ten families. We stayed at this place just a week. The family I lived with consisted of an old squaw and her eighteen-year-old son, a young squaw and eight-year-old son and an old Indian. I think they were both his wives. He was the very Indian who killed both my parents. My brother told him so and he did not deny it. They had most of our clothing in their tent even to my mother's dress and father's hymn book. One day the young squaw put on my mother's dress, a dark green woolen one, and it just about fitted her. I looked at her and then laid down on the ground and burst out crying. I could not bear to see her. She seemed to know what I was crying about and took it off. She never put on any of my mother's clothes again while I was with her. The old Indian, his young wife and her son treated me well, but the old squaw and her son were mean to me.

Wednesday morning the old squaw woke me at daybreak, she gave me a tin pail and pointed toward a mud slough not far west of us. She wanted me to get some water, but I felt tired and sleepy and did not want to go. Seeing two Indian girls of about my size playing, I put the pail down beside them and pointed to the slough, but they shook their heads. They did not want to go either. The old squaw saw that the water was not coming, picked up a stick and came after me. I started to run, but just then the young squaw came out and took in the situation at a glance. She got a big corn stalk and gave the old squaw a terrible beating. Another young squaw came up and tried to take the corn stalk away from her but she, too, got a whipping. I really felt sorry for the old squaw, but it also convinced me that the young squaw was my friend. She made the old squaw get the water herself.

Wednesday after breakfast I thought I would investigate my surroundings and find out where I was. Close to our tent was a large house with a porch on the west side. A little ways east of the building on a hill was a white house. In this house lived an Indian family with ten children. It was the largest Indian family I ever saw and most of them were small. The oldest of this family was a sixteen-year-old girl. Her face, hands, and feet were all covered with sores. I was afraid of her and whenever I saw her coming I would run away and hide. The youngest was a boy of about three years. He was a nice little fellow. He used to wear a calico shirt and string of beads around his neck. We played together by the hour. He talked Indian and I German, but we got along nicely. One day he came to visit me. He had forgotten to put on his shirt and wore only his string of beads, but he was a welcome visitor nevertheless.

Not far south from this building on the hill was a small white house surrounded by a high garden fence. At this place was a white woman. I suppose she was a captive, too. Often she would look over the fence at me, but she never came outside the gate. At the other house were five or six little white children ranging form two to ten years of age. They were English. The oldest boy spoke to me and said that the Indians would kill me. Then he spoke in Indian, *Sioux nepo nea*. I understood and shook my head as much as to say that they had not killed me yet. About noon that day they disappeared, and I never saw them again while I was prisoner.

The houses occupied by Indians and five or six families lived in tents. On a small hill south of us was a raised platform five or six feet high, on which were two coffins. While we lived there they dug a hole and buried both bodies in one grave. When an Indian dies his body is placed in a long box and a shawl is tied over the top of the box. Then it is placed on a high platform until the body is completely decomposed or for about six weeks when it is finally buried.

## Chapter IV

### *Henrietta*

Thursday morning a little white girl of four or five years was brought to our camp. I presume from the main camp about three miles distant. She was German and said her name was Henrietta but could tell nothing about herself. I was very glad to have her company. She lived with the family in the next tent to ours. Friday and Saturday we played together all day and soon were fast friends.

The first Sunday after my capture was the loneliest I have ever spent. Henrietta did not come to see me, and I sat down thinking of the previous Sunday. I wondered what a change the week had brought. Where were the people now who had been at our church and Sunday school last Sunday? Were they all in heaven with the wings of angels? Would Mr. Mannweiler hold Sunday school in heaven and distribute the pretty red cards? Thus my childish thoughts ran. Suddenly I thought of my father's hymn book. I found it and in turning over the leaves I came upon the old familiar hymn beginning, "How tedious and gloomy the hours." I knew it by heart and sang:

> Wie lange und schwer wird die Zeit,
> Wenn Jesus so lange nicht hier:
> Die Blumen, die Voegel, die Freud,
> Verlieren ihre Schoenheit zu mir.[18]

I sang the hymn about half through and then my feelings overcame me and I laid down the book and had the longest and bitterest cry since my parents had been murdered.

Besides the incidents already related, I remember nothing of interest until the moving of our camp. I think it was on Tuesday that the Indians woke me up early. They had breakfast in a hurry after which the tents were taken down and everything loaded on the wagons. Then began the moving. Of all the wild racing I ever saw this was the wildest. The Indians from the main camp caught up with us just as we were crossing the Redwood river. The stream was badly swollen on account of the big rains the week before. The Indians all got off the wagons and waded through. I screamed when the old squaw grabbed me by the arm and pulled me off the load and made me wade. She held me by the arm or I would have perished, as the water was nearly up to my arms. Just after we had crossed the river I saw one of our former neighbors, Mrs. Inefeld, with her baby. She was the first white prisoner I recognized. I spoke to her and she knew me at once. She smiled and asked me how many of our family had been killed. I answered that I thought they all were dead but myself as the Indians had told me they had cut the throats of my brother and sister because they cried. The next day, however, to my delight and surprise, I saw them both. That day I also saw Mary Schwandt and Augusta Lenz standing by the wagon and met Mrs. Urban and her five children.[19]

I wish I could describe this move as it should be described and do justice to it. Most of the teams were oxen hitched to wagons, a few horses and the rest Indian ponies with poles tied to their sides. These poles were tied together behind and loaded with household goods. They did not travel on roads as we do, but rushed across the prairie broadcast. U. S. flags, striped shawls, and bed sheets were floating in the breeze side by side. The handsomest shawls made the best saddle blankets. Clock and watch wheels the best headdresses, the most expensive jewels bedecked the Indian's breast. I have never seen a Fourth of July parade or a ragamuffin outfit equal this move.

All day I was studying the new styles and for a while forgot all my troubles. I was completely carried away by the wild scene. Even the Indians with their guns pointing at me did not frighten me. I would shut my eyes and think it would not take long to die that way, but O, those horrid butcher knives! I could not bear the sight of them and they were always sharpening them.

We camped in one large camp that night when we stopped. There must have been a thousand tents and it looked like a large city on the prairie. Henrietta and I were again companions, for her tent was next to mine as before. We started out to find some playmates and found those already mentioned. I also saw my sister did not recognize me in one short week. The Indians had put one of my baby sister's dresses on her. I asked her whose dress she had on and she said it was Bertha's. My brother was yoking a pair of oxen as we came up to him. He was delighted to see me, as the Indians had told him they had killed me for trying to run away. He told me with tears in his eyes that the Indians had killed our cow, "Molly," and could not bear to see our cattle killed, as it was all there was left of our home. Just then an Indian girl with whom Henrietta lived came and took us home.

We stayed at this place about three days. In the evening, young braves would dress in their gala attire with their clock-wheel headdresses on and would mount their ponies and practice riding and shooting on horseback. Sometimes they would hang on the side of the ponies and ride at full gallop, yelling as only an Indian knows how. Henrietta and I would sit and watch them and wonder how many Indians there were in the world. I told her it was full of them as they had killed all the white people, and so it did seem to me just then.

The evening before we moved, an old Indian walked around from tent to tent calling out something I could not understand. I went to one of the white women to find out what he said and she said we were to move early the next morning and those of the prisoners that were not able to travel were to be shot. I was badly frightened, but I was saved after all.

The next morning we moved. Little Henrietta and I rode the same wagon. As we were riding along a voice in the train behind us called out in German, "Say, you have Lettou's oxen hitched to Mannweiler's wagon." Looking back I saw a boy whom I knew, Ludwig Kitzmann.[20] Then Henrietta called out, "Why, there is Ludwig." Now I had a clue to Henrietta's identity. I called back to him, "Here is a little girl you know. I don't know who she is and I wish you would tell me." Ludwig then ran forward to our wagon, and when he came up to us he said in great astonishment, "Why, it is Henrietta Krieger, my dear little cousin."[21] After a few minutes' conversation he went back to his wagon, promising to come back again at noon yet. Her father and some of her brothers and sisters had been killed and her mother badly wounded.

Ludwig came at noon and we had an enjoyable visit. I asked him if we would always have to stay with the Indians and he told me not to worry about that as there were enough white men left to shoot off every Indian's head. I told him I wanted to run away but did not know which way to go. "Don't try that," he said, "or you will be killed. You are too little. The best thing you can do is to stay with them until the whites come and take us." I asked him where they would take us and he replied that he was going to his aunt in Wisconsin. When I told him that we did not have any relatives in this country he cheered me up the best he could and assured me that we would find friends somewhere that would take care of us.

Soon after this I was taken sick and lost all account of the days. It must be borne in mind that at this time I was only seven years old. To those who may be inclined to question the accuracy of my memory of the incidents that I have related, I can only say that many of my old fellow prisoners fully corroborate my statements. The nature of these incidents impressed them on my youthful mind so deeply that I can never forget them. It is very common that incidents occurring in our childhood are better remembered than others happening in our maturity.

While I was sick the master of our tent was absent for four or five days. His big boy took particular pains to torture and abuse me. One evening he was sitting in the tent and throwing corn cobs at me while his old mother was keeping up the fire and laughing at me. The young squaw was outside. I stood it as long as I could and then I screamed as hard as I could. All at once the young squaw stepped in and caught him in the act. She seized a large ox whip and gave him a most unmerciful threshing and he cried like a baby. Then she gathered up all the corn cobs and brought them to me. She put one in my hand and motioned for me to throw it at him. I did so with all the strength I had. Every time I threw a cob the young squaw would laugh and the boy cried. That was the time I got satisfaction even if I was in an Indian camp.

One morning the big boy brought my breakfast but as I was about to eat it he jerked it away and said I needed no breakfast for in a little while a man was coming to shoot me. The young squaw was out of doors and the rascal could act as mean toward me as he pleased. I did not believe a word he said, but after breakfast an Indian did come in with a new gun. I was so frightened that I did not recognize him. Shutting my eyes I lay down, hardly alive. He came to me and said, "How do you do," half a dozen times before I dared open my eyes. Then I saw it was the man of the tent and I presume he knew nothing of what the boy had told me. The new gun probably belonged to some dead soldier.

Another time when the young squaw went visiting I got lonesome and decided to find my brother and see him awhile. I found him together with August Gluth and Ludwig Kitzmann in a patch of hazel brush picking nuts.[22] They gave me some and while we were talking together the big boy approached us. "There comes that big Indian boy after you," said my brother. "See, he is picking up a stick to take you home. Don't you worry; we will take him home." Each of the boys picked up a stick and started for the boy. They said to him, *pokajee*, (leave). He scolded awhile but turned about and started for his tepee.

The boys took me home and when we got there the old squaw scolded a while at the boys and they laughed at her and called her "old crooked mouth" in German. When they left they told me if she or the boy whipped me to let them know and they would whip them both. After the boys had gone, the big Indian boy kicked me in the face and made my nose bleed. The young boy was at home and I think he told his mother for after that she would take me along when she went visiting.

## Chapter V
### *A Sacred Feast*

The next morning after this incident I heard a great commotion again. On investigation I saw a most disgusting spectacle. Side by side, with their throats cut and their feet in the air, lay a number of dogs. I returned to the tent sickened by the sight, but in a little while my curiosity got the better of my sensations and I went out again. By this time the Indians were singeing the hair off the dogs with burning hay. I recognized our little white poodle among the carcasses. The Indians had eight or ten kettles on the fire and as soon as a dog was singed it was thrown into the boiling water. Perhaps they were only scalding them preparatory to cooking.

I concluded they were cooking without preparation and resolved not to eat any of the meat if I had to starve. The men were about the kettles for several hours, the squaws not daring to come near. At last the women and children were driven out of the tent and only the men partook of the dog feast. Even the boys, to their great dissatisfaction, were not allowed to participate. We had to stay out until after midnight. For three nights they kept up their dog feast in adjoining tents. I have heard since that they were religious feasts and indulged in only by warriors who on this occasion were preparing for battle.

After the feasts were over all the warriors left camp on another murdering expedition. There were only old men, women, and children left to guard the prisoners.

One morning, soon after the Indians had gone, I saw a man dressed in white man's clothes. He was about the same height of my father and walked like him. For a moment I forgot everything and ran to meet him. When I came up to him I saw that it was not my father and threw myself on the ground and cried as if my heart would burst. He sat down beside me and tried to lift me up, but I refused to be comforted. After regaining my speech I told him, "Indian nepo papa and mama and I want to go *taha mea tepee*" (far away to my home)." He sympathized with me for there were tears in his eyes as he spoke to me. He asked me where my tepee was and I pointed it out to him. He took me by the hand and led me there.

That afternoon two young girls came to our tent and took me with them. They must have been half-breeds as their complexions were much lighter than the other Indians and they lived much better. I think that George Spencer, the man whom I had seen that morning, sent them to get me. This family consisted of an old squaw, a young man and two young girls. They all treated me very kindly, in fact, made a pet of me. The young man would paint my face in their fashion and allow me to look at myself in his hand glass, but as soon as I could get out of doors I would rub off the paint. Their conduct toward me was so considerate that I really liked them.

Once while with them there was a dance in camp. The young man painted my face in the highest style of Indian art and took me and his sister to see the performance. He put me on his shoulder and carried me the greater part of the way. At the dance ground a lot of poles were planted. Some with red shawls tied to them, some with white bed sheets, and some with American flags attached to them. There were no scalps in sight. The dancers stood in groups and jumped up and down while others galloped wildly about on horseback. I was afraid they would run over one another but they managed their horses very skillfully. My young Indian friend held me up on his shoulder so that I could have a fair view of the whole performance.

After a week spent with this kind family I went to live with another consisting of an old squaw (a widow), a young man and a little girl of my size. The young man was a half-breed whom I had known before the outbreak. His family had camped in our woods in the spring of 1862. He came to our house one evening and father asked him in for supper. While they were eating he asked father if he could borrow our oxen. After consulting mother about it father decided to go along himself with the oxen as soon as traveling would be possible. The Indian was satisfied and they stayed in our woods for two weeks more when father moved them and their household goods about twenty miles east.

The boy always seemed to think so much of my father and I have often wondered why he did not save his life, but perhaps he could not. While I lived with them I was half starved all the time and was always sickly. Once when I was very hungry I saw an Indian girl put some potatoes in hot ashes to roast and then go off to play. I could not resist the chance of procuring a square meal, even if by questionable means, so I watched and waited until I thought the potatoes were cooked and saw that the girl was at play on the other side of the tepee and then I took the potatoes back of another tent and ate them with great relish.

After I had eaten the potatoes, the Indian girl that had put the potatoes to roast, went to look for them and found them gone. She accused another Indian girl of taking them, and gave her a good whipping. Here is a case where the innocent suffered for the guilty.

The actions of the Indians were quite peculiar. Often on evenings they would gather in groups out of doors and relate tales of adventure and other stories. They would keep this up so late that one after another they would fall asleep and lie out of doors all night like cattle.

I remember well the day of the battle of Wood Lake.[23] It was near breakfast time when we heard the report of the first cannon. An old squaw, who was making a fire, jumped into the air so suddenly and violently when she heard the report that it seemed she had burned her foot and screamed something that sounded to me like *hi be-dish-kak*, and she repeated these words again and again. The same cry was heard throughout the camp. I noticed that there were no warriors in camp but did not realize that they had gone to battle.

We got little to eat that day of the battle. Everything was in the greatest confusion. They kept up bonfires all that night and an incessant howling and screaming. The next morning I changed masters again. The old squaw who kept my sister after we left the first camp was my new guardian. There were no men at this tent. There was one Indian family that often camped in our woods. The squaw used to come to our house a great deal and mother would show her how to bake bread and do a good many other things. Father used to call her mother's sister because she was such a great friend of ours. While a prisoner I met her quite often and spoke to her but she never spoke to me and acted as if she had never seen me.

About this time we moved quite frequently, but I cannot remember the particulars. One day, not long after the battle, a young squaw came to our tent in a great hurry and, after a short consultation, they began to pack up my sister's effects. All the clothes I had were on my person. Soon they started with us to a hill, or elevated place where we saw a large number of Indians standing in a circle in the center of which a white flag waved from a pole. There were a lot of prisoners entering the circle through an opening in the line and as none came out I concluded that they were going to kill all the whites so I did not want to go. Two Indian girls took and carried me in.

Here I met my brother, August Gluth, and Ludwig Kitzmann. They greeted me most joyfully. "We are going to be free now," said my brother. "The soldiers have licked the Indians and now they have to give us up." I missed Gustaf Kitzmann among the prisoners and asked for him. Mrs. Inefeld then told the story of his death. She and Gustaf were staying with the same family. He used to run away to see his brother Ludwig. The Indians did not like this. Besides this he had a bad habit of pinching Indian children and pulling their hair. The day they killed him he was crying and wanted to see his brother. The Indians would not let him go, however. They then went to sharpening their butcher knives and told her to get a pail of water. She took her baby with her. The baby often cried and they had threatened to kill it. When she came back little Gustaf was lying on the ground all cut to pieces.

They then picked up the pieces and tied them up in a tablecloth while another Indian was digging the hole to bury him in. In half an hour all was done and little Gustaf was no more.[24]

Ludwig Kitzmann, August Gluth, and my brother were always together when it was possible. They had to catch and yoke oxen for hours at a time. Most of the oxen had ropes tied around their horns by the Indians so they could manage them. One night a big rain fell. The ropes tightened around the oxen's horns and they were nearly crazed with pain. Ludwig told the Indians what ailed them and they gave the boys butcher knives and they all cut the ropes. After that the boys were kept busy driving and attending the oxen.

The boys told me what the white flag meant and I was overjoyed to think that we would soon be free. In a little while we were marched to the other side of the camp and they gave us tents which we were told to occupy until General Sibley and his soldiers arrived. Here I met quite a number of the German prisoners, among whom were little Minnie Schmidt, Mary Schwandt, Augusta Lentz, Mrs. Inefeld and her baby, Mrs. Lammers and her two children, Mrs. Lang and two children, Mrs. Frass and three children, Mrs. Urban and five children.[25]

The last three ladies that I have mentioned were sisters—Mrs. Eisenreich and her five children.[26] I asked Mrs. Eisenreich what made Peter's and Sophy's heads sore and they told me that the Indians hit them on the back of their heads with a tomahawk because they could not walk any faster when they came into camp. The back of their heads was one big scab. It made me sick to look at them. Mrs. Krause and her two children, [and] Pauline Krause (Mr. Krause's sister), were missing, and another girl by the name of Henrietta Nichols (a cousin of Augusta Lentz) could not be found.[27]

These two girls were about twelve years old. Mrs. Krause said that they were hid among the Indians and that the soldiers should find them or she would never go until they were found. When the soldiers came she told them about it. They told her that they would find them, and so they did, two weeks later in another Indian camp. I remember how the soldiers cheered them when they came. When we reached St. Peter, Henrietta Nichols found her father.[28] How pleased she was to see him. Her mother and brother had been killed. Here I met Minnie Schmidt.[29] She was from our neighborhood and it was with them we stayed the first month we were in Minnesota. Minnie and I had always been great friends.

I went to where she sat and asked her if the Indians had killed all her people. She nodded her head but did not speak. Her bright blue eyes filled with tears in a moment. I tried to cheer her up and offered her one of my sweet crackers that Mrs. Urban had given me, for I thought I had offended her. She shook her head and would not take it. The tears started to my eyes for I did not know what to do and I did not want Minnie to be angry with me. Then Mrs. Krause came and told me that Minnie could not speak as there was something wrong with her throat.

I stayed with her until noon when Mrs. Krause came and told me to go and play, saying as I went, "Minnie Schmidt will soon be an angel." I did not quite understand and said, "Why, Minnie is so good that she is an angel now." Mrs. Krause replied, "Yes, she will soon die and go to heaven." Minnie rallied a little and lived three weeks longer until we reached Fort Ridgely, where she [was] turned over to that kind nurse, Mrs. Elizabeth Muller, Dr. Muller's wife, who stayed at the fort. She took care of the sick and wounded and closed many dying eyes. She also closed Minnie Schmidt's, for two days later she died.

## Chapter VI
### *The Stars of Hope*

We waited three days for the arrival of the soldiers. In the forenoon of the third day. Pauline Urban, my little sister Amelia and I were playing in a wagon when Pauline all at once jumped into the wagon seat, clapped her hands and pointed toward the south, exclaimed, "Look at the stars! Look at the stars!" We all looked in that direction and we could plainly see the sun shining on the soldier's bayonets as they marched along. Stars of hope they seemed for all of us. We got on the wagon seat or as high as we could get, to see the soldiers. At last the officers rode into camp and there was a great deal of hand shaking between them and the chiefs. I thought they knew but little of how they treated us.

The prisoners were now turned over to the soldiers and we were marched to their camp. Just as we reached the soldier's camp the sun went down. The soldiers cheered us when we reached camp, but it frightened me. I thought the Indians were trying to drive them back.

My sister and I were sent to the same tent with several others. We were nearly starved as we had eaten almost nothing all that day. There were between ninety and a hundred prisoners, and it was no easy task to furnish them all with supper. My sister and I were so small that the soldiers overlooked us but we were fortunate enough, however, to be able to share supper with some of our fellow prisoners. We stayed with the soldiers three weeks and as rations were getting scarce and what there was, was almost unfit to eat, we children were always looking for something to eat.

In the northern part of the soldiers' camp there was a German baker who used to bake very nice bread. One day we found the place and made him a visit. He treated us to a dish of beef soup and some bread. The next day we repeated our visit but he did not treat us again. Shortly after this we made the acquaintance of a boy named Ben Juni. He was more of a ladies' man and whenever Ben got anything good to eat he would divide with us. Pauline always said he was the best boy in the lot. But I could not go back on my brother and Ludwig Kitzmann. I have never seen any of my little friends of years ago and I have often wished that time could turn back in its flight and we could meet again. How much I would give to see the bright and happy face of Pauline Urban.

Henrietta Krieger was entirely forgotten after I made Pauline's acquaintance. Her mother was with her. She had four sisters and brothers. She told me she was going to meet her father soon for he was away some place where he was safe. She was about the age of my sister whom the Indians had killed. How I envied her. Her father, mother, sisters and brothers were alive and well, while mine were dead. She could always cheer me no matter how badly I felt. Her mother treated me and my sister as kindly as she did her own children.

While we stayed at Camp Release I heard some of saddest stories I ever heard. These stories were told in English and were translated to me by Mary Schwandt.[30]

Mrs. Adams told the following story. They were moving to Hutchinson when the Indians overtook them. The Indians shot at them and they jumped off the wagon. Her husband was wounded and got away, but she supposed he was killed. Then they took her baby from her arms and dashed its brains out on the wagon wheel. She was taken prisoner. She laughed while telling her story and she said she could not cry for her child. I regarded her as a brute and always hated her after that.

Mrs. Minnie Inefeld told how she went to her brother's house to tell them that the Indians were killing everybody. She left her husband loading up their household goods. When she returned she found her husband lying on the floor with a butcher knife in his heart.

One day while she was staying at Camp Release, Mr. Thiele came into our tent. He told Mrs. Krause how the Indians had killed his wife and child. He assured her that her husband was alive and that she would soon see him again. Then he went on talking about how he and a half-breed, Mooer, buried the dead. They buried quite a number before he had courage enough to go and bury his wife and child. When he came to their bodies the dogs had eaten most of them and there was nothing left but a few pieces of their clothes. He said he knelt down beside them and cried, prayed and cursed the Indians, all in one breath. He swore that he would shoot Indians all the rest of his life. At last the half breed could stand it no longer and asked Thiele if he was going to kill him, too. Mr. Thiele did not answer at which Mooer threw down his spade and went away, leaving him to bury his dead alone.

After burying what dead he could that day, he started for the fort, not caring when he went. With nothing to eat but corn and wild plums, he wandered until he met Sibley's men. He asked the General to let him have some soldiers to bury the dead. General Sibley could not send a force until two weeks later and then there was nothing left of the bodies but the bones and clothes. They simply dug a hole beside the skeletons, rolled the bones in and covered them up.[31]

I stood Mr. Thiele's talk as long as I could and then asked him if he had buried my folks. "Who are you?" he asked. I told him I was Minnie Busse, Fred Busse's eldest girl. He shook hands with me and I sat down beside him. He kept repeating, over and over gain, "Poor Fred, Poor Fred. How hard he worked and then had to leave it all behind." Suddenly, recollecting what I had asked, he answered, "Yes, child, I think I buried them. There were five bodies we found on your father's place which we buried."

Mr. Thiele's talk made me sick.

All night I cried, and Mrs. Krause took good care of me. She told me such a nice story, in her plain, simple way, that I never can forget it. She told me that after people were dead, nothing would hurt them, as they were angels then, and that Mr. Thiele had picked out such a nice place to bury my beloved ones in; a pretty meadow where the grass would always grow green and where the prairie lilies would breathe their fragrance over the graves of the departed. And then winter will come and cover the graves with its beautiful white snow. She told me not to cry about my parents any more; every time I felt like crying, to think of the nice things she had told me. I tried my best to do as Mrs. Krause had told me and found it much better not to cry.

Soon after this we broke up camp and moved. My sister and I got in the same wagon with Hattie Adams and Mary Schwandt. When he hauled in the evening my sister and I were both asleep. Our teamster was a young boy about eighteen or nineteen years of age. He picked me up out of the wagon as though I was a baby. I screamed, as it frightened me so. He said he did not mean to frighten me. It was quite cold that evening and our clothes were very thin. I felt very cold and so bad when I found that Mary was gone, and that I would see her no more. I tried not to cry, but the tears would come anyway. Our young friend, the teamster, was a German, and he felt very bad for us. He baked us some pancakes and made some coffee.

After supper he built a fire, got the blanket from the wagon and put it around us both and told us to sit there until he fed his oxen. I sat there awhile and finally getting tired of waiting, I started to look up my new acquaintance and his ox team. To my surprise, I found one of the oxen was our black ox, Billy. I told the teamster about it and he put his arms around Billy's neck. My new friend, the teamster, laughed and told me that Billy was a lazy ox, but he was going to use him better since he had learned his history. When his work was done he came back to the fire. We found a man sitting on a log by the fire watching my sleeping sister. My young friend told me it was his sister's husband.

They both talked a long while about us. The new arrival asked me a great many questions about my people and where we lived. Finally he said he thought my father was alive. The soldiers had picked up a man near New Ulm, badly wounded, who had walked many miles after he was shot and he thought that probably it was my father. I thought of what Thiele had said about burying my parents and told him of it. He told me that Thiele had buried so many dead that he may have made a mistake. I wish he had never told me this, as it only gave me false hopes, and when I found out the truth it made me feel more disappointed.

## Chapter VII
## *On the Road to St. Peter*

The next morning we started for the fort. After an early breakfast a teamster took and put me in his wagon. While we were waiting for some women and children to come to the wagon I told our new teamster that I had a brother among the prisoners and wished he could go along too. He consented, and as my brother came along just then he asked him. My brother answered that he was in no great hurry to get to St. Peter and would rather stay with the ox teams. I tried my best to get him to come, but he would not. He called me a cry baby and said I always wanted something. If we would have known then that we were not to meet again for two long years, our farewell would have been more affectionate.

Among those who rode on our wagon were Ludwig Kitzmann, Mrs. Urban, and Mrs. Krause with their children, an American lady with two children and a boy about eight or nine years old. It was very cold that morning, the wind blowing a perfect gale. Our teamster took off his overcoat and gave it to my sister and me to cover ourselves up with. The little American boy was shivering from the cold and tried to get under the coat, too. I would not allow that, however, and slapped him in the face. That was too much for Ludwig Kitzmann and he told me I was the meanest girl he had ever seen. I did feel ashamed of myself and offered the boy the coat, but the teamster settled the difficulty by giving him a horse blanket.

All that day we traveled and passed many deserted houses with nice gardens, but no living thing in sight. Even the few hardy flowers that were left in the gardens looked sad and forsaken as we passed by. How desolate everything seemed. In the evening we stopped at a deserted farm house. There [were] a lot of stables around it and the log house looked something like ours did. My sister thought we were home when she saw the house.

When we got inside she looked around and asked, "Where [are] father and mother?" I was obliged to tell her the whole sad truth, that we would never see our parents again. She cried so hard that the teamster picked her up and carried her to sleep.

The next morning we started out early as they wanted to reach Fort Ridgely that day. There were five or six horse teams which took the women and children. The rest of the teams stayed behind and got to the fort later. Everything went well until about noon, when all at once we heard shooting over the hill ahead of us. The teams all stopped and everything was in the greatest confusion. Some of the women and children wanted to run for the woods. Everybody was crying, some were praying, and others were cursing.

Just then we saw about forty Indians running for the very woods the women had been wanting to run to. One of the teamsters ventured to say that there were soldiers beyond the hill or the Indians would not be running, and so it proved, for just then a lot of soldiers appeared over the hill on horseback.

One horse was carrying two soldiers. The officers said that they had met the Indians and had exchanged a few shots with them, resulting in the killing of one of the soldiers' horses. While the officer was talking one of the women cried out, "O, look! There comes a whole army of Indians." We all looked in that direction she was pointing, and sure enough, there were a lot of men on horseback. It seemed like a large cloud of dust coming in our direction like a whirlwind. We could not tell whether they were soldiers or Indians, but as they turned out to be soldiers, we were all happy to see them. They had been out scouting and, hearing the shooting, came to see what the trouble was. After the excitement had died down no one seemed to care for anything to eat so we resumed our journey to the fort.

About an hour after starting we saw a lone man coming across the prairie toward us. As he came nearer Ludwig exclaimed, "It is Mr. Gluth!" and jumped off the wagon and ran toward him. He spoke with the man about something for quite a while, at which the man dropped on the ground and cried like a baby. Some of the men went to see what the trouble was and found out that he was the father of August Gluth, a little ten-year-old boy who had been taken prisoner by the Indians, and that this was the first news he had received that his son was alive.

Before we reached Fort Ridgely a man driving an ox team caught up with us and took Mrs. Lammers and her two children with him. She was the first prisoner we parted with on the road and many of the women cried when they bade her good-bye. Afterwards I heard that the man was Mr. Rieke and that he married Mrs. Lammers.

At last we reached the fort, tired and hungry. The soldiers marched us into the dining room where supper was already waiting for us. Soldiers were standing everywhere behind the chairs to see that every little child had something to eat. It was the first time in ten long weeks that we had eaten at a table like civilized people. When supper was over they took us to another room where they made up some beds on the floor for us.

The next morning they did not wake us as early as usual. After breakfast some of us children begged Mrs. Krause to let us see Minnie Schmidt. She had been turned over to Mrs. Miller for treatment. She consented to take us and when we arrived at the hospital we found Minnie lying on a nice clean bed with her hair curled as nice as her mother used to curl it. She opened her blue eyes one moment and smiled. Then she closed them again as if too tired to keep them open. How bad we felt and all commenced to cry. The lady who stood at the head of the bed motioned for us to go. It was the last we saw of little Minnie, for two days later she died and her troubles were ended.

When we got back the teams were already waiting for us and we started for St. Peter. On our way to St. Peter we could see people in the field at work here and there and also a few herds of cattle were grazing in the meadow. One place we passed, a man was waving his hat and calling to us. The team stopped to [ask] what we wanted. Presently two men with milk came up while the man who stopped us was carrying a lot of tin cups. The teamster cheered the men as they came and told them that it was the greatest treat they could give us for so many children had asked for milk. How greedily we drank it and the men smiled as they watched us and said they were sorry that they had no more.

That evening we reached St. Peter, where we were turned loose in an empty store. A fire was burning here which was a most welcome sight as we were cold. Some kind person had carried in a few armfuls of hay for us to sleep on. We had little for supper. The town was full of people who had fled from their homes and not yet returned.

The next morning people came crowding in, bright and early, to look for friends. No one seemed to think of breakfast. Mr. Lang was one of the first to come in. His wife and two children stood just opposite the door. He walked over to her and took the baby from her arms. I never saw a more joyful meeting in my life. Those who had no friends were all crying. There was hardly a dry eye in the house. Mary Reyff came in next, dressed in the deepest of mourning. She looked over the crowd and never spoke a word. Sadly she turned to the door and walked out, having found none of her people. She was working out away from home, and her folks had been killed, including her lover. Afterwards she found two elder brothers who escaped. I held my sister by the hand as I was afraid someone in the crowd might take her away, and I would not know what had become of her.

People were still coming to claim friends who were supposed to be dead. I could not help watching the door and thinking of the story the teamster had told me, but it was in vain—my father and mother never came.

At last the crowd was beginning to thin out; Reverend Friedrich Emde of the Evangelical Church touched me on the should and said that he would take me. I told him I had a little sister with me and wanted him to take her also. Mrs. Emde then came to us and took off her veil and tied it around my sister's head and a little shawl around mine. While I was waiting for them to leave with us, I looked once more over the crowd.

In one corner lay Ludwig Kitzmann talking to a man and boy and in the other corner sat the little brown-faced boy of whom I have spoken before. He looked so sad and no one seemed to notice him. Often I have wondered what became of him. Mrs. Inefeld was looking out of the window with tears in her eyes holding her baby so close to her. Her husband and all her folks had been killed and there was no one to claim her. Henrietta Krieger found her mother afterwards. How pleased she was to see her.

At last Mr. and Mrs. Emde were ready to go. They first took us to a house where we had breakfast, after which we went to a store to get some shoes and stockings. Mr. Emde told him our story, at which he said he would make us a present of what we wanted. When we were dressed as comfortable as they could make us we started for New Ulm. It was about noon when we left and did not stop until we reached a farmhouse that evening. The next day we reached John Muhs, a brother of Mrs. Emde, who lived six miles south of New Ulm. Mr. and Mrs. Muhs were my parents for the next two years, and my sister stayed with Mrs. Emde.

I told Mr. Emde of my brother and he promised that he would look for him when he went back to St. Peter. He found out that my brother had been picked up in St. Paul by another minister and later was sent to a family near Hutchinson. The man who took my brother was appointed our guardian and received quite a sum of money, about $1,200 for my father's personal property. This was too much for him to let go. As soon as he had everything settled as he wanted it, he came to Mr. Muhs and Mr. Emde asked him to give me and my sister up to him, as he was well off and would adopt us. Finally, Mr. Muhs consented and turned us over to him.

When we got to our new house we soon found out that our guardian owned nothing but a farm which he had bought with the money he so cunningly appropriated. As for schooling, we saw but little of it. I do not wish to speak unkindly of my guardian, as he really did not abuse me and I think he would have done what was right, but he was not well and his wife was the head of the family. They both have passed away since, and I will not judge them now. Of my father's property we never received one cent.

When I was fifteen years old I started out in the world to earn my own living. I worked out summers and went to school winters. Being able to read German, in time I received a fair education. In 1879, I married Owen Carrigan and am mother of five children. My husband died in 1898. As to my sister Amelia, she left our guardian at the age of fourteen and went back to Reverend Emde. She is now Mrs. Reynolds of Minneapolis.

My brother left for Montana at the age of nineteen. When we were at Camp Release he came one day and told me that he saw all the Indians were to be hung but the one who killed our parents was not among them. He cried and said, "Yes, he is a good Indian now. Just wait until I get big I will hunt Indians the rest of my life and will kill them, too, if I can find them." For two years after we parted he would write to me regularly, but then we heard that he was killed at the time General Custer made his last stand, for that spring I received his last letter.[32]

There are only three places that I would like to see again. One is the large flat lime rock on the bank of the Minnesota River where my brother and I used to go fishing. Years have passed and many a person has claimed my white rock since. The Indians that used to pass us in their canoes so silently they seemed like ghosts, you could hardly hear the dip of their oars, have long since fled from the bank of the river, and could not frighten now.

The second place is the spring near my father's place where my playmates and I used to pick the yellow lady slipper. The third is the creek near our house where the lovely white cherry blossoms were so thick that they looked like a white sheet. Little Pauline and Minnie Kitzmann, my sister Augusta and I brought our aprons full home to make garlands out of them. Years after when I used to see the white cherry blossoms I used to wish that I could go back and cover the graves of my little friends with the flowers they loved so well.

The flowers that bloom in the wildwood
Have since dropped their beautiful leaves,
And the many dear friends of my childhood
Have slumbered for years in their graves.

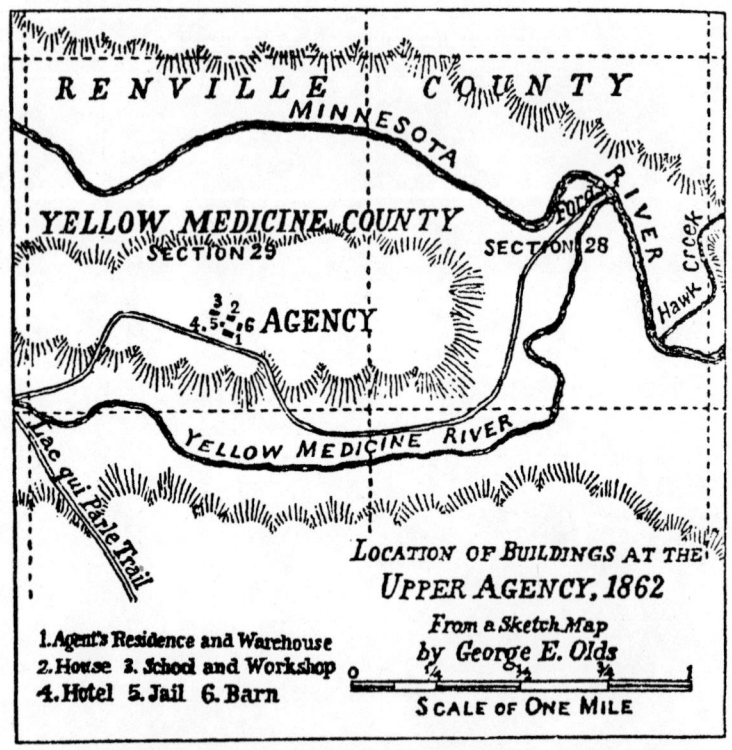

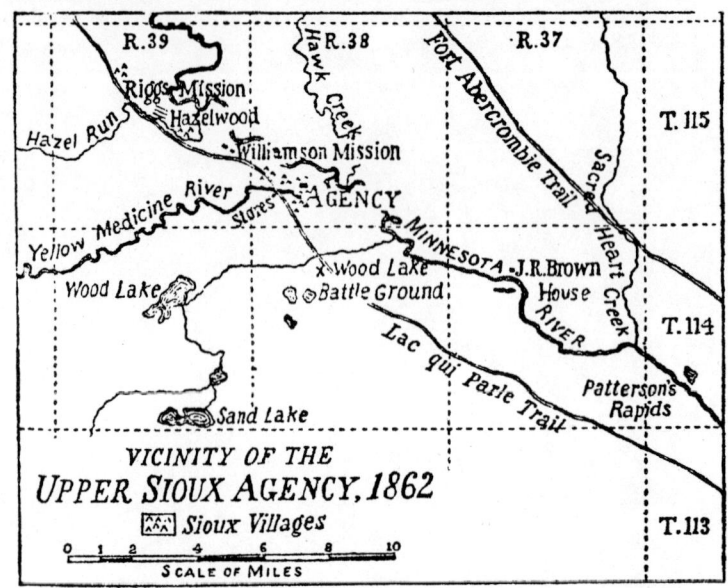

60 / GERMAN PIONEER ACCOUNTS OF THE GREAT SIOUX UPRISING OF 1862

**LOCATION OF BUILDINGS AT THE UPPER AGENCY, 1862**

*From a Sketch Map by George E. Olds*

1. Agent's Residence and Warehouse
2. House  3. School and Workshop
4. Hotel  5. Jail  6. Barn

SCALE OF ONE MILE

**VICINITY OF THE UPPER SIOUX AGENCY, 1862**

Sioux Villages

SCALE OF MILES

From *A History of Minnesota* by William Watts Folwell

# *Other Related Reminiscences*
## —by Minnie Bruce Carrigan

### *The Negro Godfrey*

*T*HERE WAS A NEGRO AMONG THE INDIANS named Joe Godfrey.[1] I heard he was brought from St. Louis by John Faribo. After John Faribo died he went to live with his son Oliver Faribo, who was an Indian trader living at Shakopee. The first time I saw this Negro was while I was a prisoner. I used to wonder why his hair was black and curly and his face black, and the Indians' faces brown and their hair straight. One evening I was sitting by Mrs. Inefeld. He was riding a beautiful white pony and was dressed in a soldier's coat, with a red leather belt around his waist, and a silk stovepipe hat on, with Indian leggings and moccasins, and his breast was covered with all kinds of jewelry.

I was asked by my friend, Mrs. Inefeld, what made him look so different from the Indians. She told me that he was a Negro and that he was more brutal than the Indians were. She said that he bragged about killing seventeen women and children near New Ulm in one day, and how they begged for their lives.[2] The breastpins he was wearing he had stolen from the women he had murdered.

Mrs. Inefeld said that it was too bad that such a beautiful white horse should be made to carry such a vile brute. She told me to keep out of his reach as far as I could. I hear he is still living on the Swantee Indian reservation. He is married to his second Indian wife, a young girl, seventeen years old, thereby becoming a ward of the government, or is sponging on his wife's allowance.

At the time of the massacre he turned state's evidence to save his own neck, and sent many of the Indians to the gallows. It is claimed by good authority that even now he brags of killing a man and his wife and roasting their child in an oven near New Ulm in 1862.[3] He dare not leave the reservation for fear of the white people shooting him. It is a pity the Indians do not shoot him for being a cowardly sneak thief, if the white people cannot get a chance. It is a pity that such a brute should be allowed to pollute the earth.

## The Story of Emanuel Reyff
Written by Minnie Buce Carrigan
Told by Emanuel Reyff

We moved from Helenville, Jefferson County, Wisconsin, in the spring of 1862 and settled at Middle Creek, Minnesota. We filed on our claim and went on breaking up the sod. We had settled at Forest City, Minnesota, two years previous. Monday, August 18, I was working on the Minnesota River, driving rafting logs down to New Ulm for the sawmill. The boss said the river was too low so we could not go down. So he paid us off and I started to go to my brother, Eusebius, with whom I then lived.[4]

A friend of mine named Bill Laur went with me. We went together as far as the hill at Beaver Creek and then parted. He went to New Ulm, where his folks lived and I went to my brother's. Just as I was coming to the cow yard the Indians were coming from the opposite direction to the house. My brother and his son Ben, a boy ten years of age, were stacking hay near the house. One of the Indians shot at my brother with an arrow. It struck him under the jaw bone near the ear. As he fell from the load the Indians grabbed him, cut off both his hands and scalped him before he was dead.

Ben jumped off the stack and tried to escape, but there were about forty Indians and poor little Ben had no show. One of the Indians grabbed him by the hair and held him while the other Indian dumped off the hay rack, which was nearly empty, turned up the wagon tongue and tied Ben's feet together with a rope and hung him to the wagon tongue by this heels. They then cut his pants off with a butcher knife and slashed up his body as only an Indian knows. Then they poured powder over his body and set in on fire. He died quickly. I thanked God when he was dead. They scalped him, also. He was such a fat little fellow and they seemed to like the job.

My sister-in-law came out of the house and begged on her knees for her life. An Indian rudely seized her by the hair and held her while the other Indians drove four stakes into the ground and then tied her to them: then they mutilated her body with butcher knives. After she was dead they scalped her, too.

Little Annie rushed out of the house screaming with fright. Two squaws grabbed her by the arms and cut her to pieces with butcher knives on the door step. When the first shooting commenced I climbed a tree that was covered with a grape vine near the cow yard. From my hiding place I could see all that was passing, but dared not move. Twice I drew my revolver to shoot. Once when they tied my sister-in-law to the stake, and when they cut up little Ben. But it was only one against forty Indians, and it would have given them another victim if I had revealed my hiding place.

As soon as the killing was all done the Indians passed right under the tree I was hiding in and went to the Kochendorfer place, our next neighbor's. I climbed out of the tree and ran as fast as I could to the Schmidt's place. Here I saw one of the most horrible sights I ever witnessed in my life. Mrs. Schmidt's head was lying on the table with a knife and fork stuck in it. They had cut off one of her breasts and laid it on the table beside the head and put her baby nursing the other breast. The child was still alive.

The dog they had killed on the doorstep. I ran out of the house as quickly as I ran into it and ran down to the Minnesota River, right below Schmidt's house, for there were a whole lot of Indians coming over the bluff and they had not yet discovered me. I swam the river and started for Fort Ridgely, but there were so many Indians around the fort I changed my course and went to New Ulm and got there just before it was attacked by the Indians and helped to defend the town during the siege. My nephew, Eusebius, was working near New Ulm, and my nieces, Mary and Emma, were both away at work. I found all of them and told them the sad news of their parents' and Annie's death. It was a hard story for me to tell them.

My nephew and I both enlisted in Company K, the Seventh Minnesota. We were sent to help bury the dead. We commenced near New Ulm and it took us three weeks before we got to my brother's place. We found the bones of the four bodies and buried them in one grave near the garden. Our lieutenant was with us. Afterward we were detailed to guard the thirty-eight Indians at the hanging at Mankato. There were nine names called out to place the ropes around the Indians' necks. My name was among them and I performed the task with pleasure. Afterward we were sent south and I helped fight thirty-two battles including the Indian war.

The Reyff family lived about one mile and a half from our home. They had not lived there very long. We used to meet at Sunday school. The Sunday before the outbreak we met at Sunday school and walked part way home together. When we parted that day we did not know that that day was the last time we would ever meet: that the next day three of us six would be killed, and that my sister, Ben and Annie would be the victims.

While I was a prisoner with the Indians and they were moving, I saw a little girl riding on a wagon with Annie Reyff's dress on. I followed her all the afternoon, thinking it was my little friend Annie, When I caught up with her I found it was a quarter blood Indian girl with Annie's dress on. I knew then that Annie must be dead or they would not have her dress. I felt so sorry and disappointed I sat down and cried.

## *The Story of J. G. Lane*

My mother was the widow of Daniel Lane. There were three of us children, my brother J. G., my sister Minnie, and myself. My mother afterward married Friedrich Krieger, a widower with four daughters.[5] The spring of 1862 we started for Minnesota. We drove through with [an] ox team and took our sheep and cattle with us, and I had to drive cattle part of the time. I was only seven years old but I remember the journey perfectly. I remember well when we reached my uncle, Paul Kitzmann, who had moved to Sacred Heart the previous year.

How glad we were when our journey ended. On Saturday evening, August 17, Louis Kitzmann, my cousin, my brother John, and I went to look for the cattle. One of the cows had a bell on but we could not hear it. We had to go clear to the river bank, about three miles. While we were at the river we could hear shooting and yelling. We thought it was Indians but saw no one. He said it was only Indians hunting.

Monday evening, August 18, Emil Grundmann and August Frass drove up to our house.[6] Each one had an ox team and they were prodding them with pitch forks to hurry them up. They told my mother that the Indians were killing everybody; that they had passed Mr. Mannweiler's place and found him dead in the door yard and Busse's place and found Mr. Busse and his wife and some of the children dead, and everything torn out of the house. They then asked where my father was, and drove on to Mr. Krause's place.

My stepfather, Mr. Krieger, and my uncle, Paul Kitzmann, were fishing at the Minnesota River. My cousin Louis was sent to call them. The whole neighborhood was soon gathered at my uncle's place to see what was to be done. My uncle had so much faith in the Indians he could not believe that they had done the killing.

He sent two men to Schwandt's house. They soon returned with the bloody coat of Schwandt's hired man, with a bullet hole in it, as evidence of their visit. They had found most of the family murdered. This convinced my uncle. Then there was a hurried gathering up of the household goods and provisions. They then hitched up the oxen and started. We traveled all night and until Tuesday morning, when all of a sudden we discovered a group of Indians on horseback upon the hill west of us. They were all armed with double barrel shotguns. After holding a short council among themselves, they made a dash for us.

When they were a short distance away from us one Indian dismounted and came toward us. He asked my uncle what they were leaving for. He replied that the Indians were killing all the white people, and that they were going to leave the country. The Indians replied that it was the Chippewas that were doing all the killing. He told us to go to our homes and that they would protect us. They were hungry and wanted something to eat. The teams all stopped.

The Indians sat down in a circle with their guns behind them. There were eight of them. My uncle gathered up some bread among the crowd and passed it around among the Indians. I have often wondered why no one in the crowd noticed the Indians' guns. My uncle could have taken all of them as he passed the bread around and the other men could have run out to meet him and each one have a gun and we would have had the brutes at our mercy.

I noticed the guns and spoke to my mother about it, but she told me to keep still. My uncle was the only man who had a gun and one of the boys had a revolver, but neither had any ammunition. We then turned about and started back to our homes. The Indians escorted us. Sometimes they would ride ahead of us and sometimes behind us, and part of the time they would be out of sight. But they were constantly watching us. This continued until we were in sight of our homes. We suddenly came upon the bodies of two dead men, one lying on each side of the road, and a dead dog.

The Indians were ahead out of sight just then. The sight of the dead bodies excited Mr. Krause, who was riding a mare that had a colt with her. He owned the only horses in the neighborhood. He suddenly bolted the track and rode over the hills east toward Fort Ridgely. I can see him yet as he passed us. His wife was screaming and everything was in confusion. Just then the Indians appeared again west of us and missed Mr. Krause. They inquired for him. No one answered. Then they went ahead a short distance and dismounted and left their ponies and came back took their position four on each side of the wagon train.

The firing commenced. Confusion reigned supreme. Everybody was screaming and flying for their lives. I saw August Guess running toward the timber near Kraus' place; my brother followed him. I jumped off the wagon and followed them. As I was running I noticed toward the right of us a group of Indians looking over the hill and watching the slaughter of our people below like so many hungry wolves watching for their prey. There must have been fifty of them. We could hear shooting and screaming as we ran. After we reached the woods we rested from our excitement. It was nearly dark.

After the massacre of our people was over, the group of Indians on the hill had joined these in the valley that had done the killing. They all marched towards the woods, where we were hiding. When they came to the timber they turned and went to my uncle's place. That was all we saw of them that night. Early the next morning we heard someone hammering as though they were repairing something. We left our hiding place and started for the noise. We saw that it was the Indians at my uncle's place. There was a great number of them. We noticed also that they had Mr. Krause's mare and colt in their position, which led us to think that Mr. Krause had been killed, but later we learned that he escaped by abandoning the animals.

While watching the proceedings of the Indians, whose ponies were grazing between them and ourselves, we noticed two of them leave the group and come toward us, which frightened us and we returned to hiding place, where we remained until night, when we went to my uncle's place, and found the coast clear. We found the cows, milked one of them, drank all the milk we could, poured the balance on the ground and hung the pail upside down on a fence post.

After looking around to see that everything was safe, we returned to our hiding place. While on the way we noticed two objects in the distance but could not distinguish what they were, for it was quite dark. We dropped into the grass, and had lain there but a short time when what we supposed were two dogs jumped over us and took no notice of us and disappeared in the darkness. We stayed a little longer and then went back to our hiding place and remained there for the night.

The next day we ventured out for something to eat. We started for Mr. Krause's house, for that was the nearest to our hiding place. Just before we reached it, we found their dog lying dead beside the path. It made us feel bad to see him. When we reached the house we found half of the floor torn up and taken away. On the other half stood a home-made table with a drawer in it for knives and forks. We opened the drawer and found half a loaf of bread. We divided it into three equal parts and ate it. Bread never tasted so good to me before.

While we were staying at our hiding place the cows came quite near us. We crept up quite carefully and caught one of them by the horns and held her while the other would milk directly into his mouth. So we took turns until we all satisfied our hunger. Then we returned to our hiding place until dark. Some time during the night we started our journey to Fort Ridgely. We traveled by night and slept daytimes. Sometimes we would get very tired. We would have to take a short rest and then travel again.

We continued this way for six nights. The last night we took the wagon track. It was a very dark night. After finding the road we walked quite a distance and came to the foot of a hill. When we started uphill again we noticed a dark cloud on the hill ahead of us. On close inspection we saw that there were objects moving. We dropped on our knees and tried to make out what it was.

We turned out of the road double-quick and dropped ourselves on the grass and remained there until they passed. It proved to be Indians and they passed us so closely we could distinguish their guns on their shoulders. We remained there a short time and then went up the hill. We turned to the right again and concluded to take a short rest. The sudden excitement had tired us out completely. We slept for a while, then started to find the road again. It was so dark we had to give it up. We dropped down in our tracks and had another sleep.

When we woke up the next morning the sun was shining in our faces. In must have been about nine o'clock and a fine morning it was. We were on the top of the hill and just below us was the fort and the beautiful stars and stripes were floating above it. What a beautiful sight it was to us half-starved children. Between us and the fort were three farm houses. We thought these houses must be occupied by people, they were so close to the fort, and we wanted something to eat. We were looking at the houses and not at the ground and we almost stepped on a dead man lying in the grass.

This frightened us so badly we left the road and struck out for the prairie again. This took us quite away from the buildings. After we had passed them we came to some cattle that belonged to our own neighborhood. We wondered how they came away down there, and my sheep was there, too. We stopped again and looked at some more cattle that we knew. I suppose that the soldiers brought them down there for beef, but I did not think of it then.

All at once we noticed a soldier waving his cap at us, then started to run toward us. When he got quite near he called out, "Hurry up, boys; you are so close to the fort, but you may be killed yet before you reach it." He took my brother by the hand and led him along. So we reached the fort in safety.

The first thing the soldiers did was to ask our names. We went by the name of Krieger at that time, so we gave our names as John and Gottlieb Krieger and August Guess. During our journey to the fort we had nothing to eat but grass and sheep sorrel. The last meal we had was when we milked the cows before we started for the fort. The first meal the soldiers gave us was a small bowl of milk and bread. My, how hungry it made us. The next day we found a barrel of crackers and helped ourselves. In a few days we were sent to St. Peter on what was called a refugee train.

It consisted of a long train of wagons and horse teams in which they placed all the refugees and sent them east. It was guarded in front and rear by cavalry, and we landed safely in St. Peter. Here we stayed a few days; then we were sent on to St. Paul and put on a boat and sent to La Crosse, Wisconsin. Here we were put on a train and sent to the nearest station to my grandmother, Mrs. Miller. The people of that town took up a collection and hired a livery team and landed us at my grandmother's door. I remained here for a while and herded her cows.

Late that fall I learned that my mother was alive, but the news seemed too good to be true, and I did not believe it. One evening my grandmother called to me to bring the cows. She was standing in the road waiting for me when a lady came up to her and spoke to her. I heard my mother's voice, but it seemed like one risen from the dead, and frightened me. We met and I was overjoyed to see her. She brought me some clothes and visited us awhile, then went back to Minnesota again. I stayed with my grandmother awhile, then to live with a family by the name of Bucholtz and went to school. I think I stayed with them a year. Then my uncle, John Kitzmann, and my cousin, Mike, moved close to Rochester, Minnesota. They took my brother and me with them.

There we had to drive cattle for the second time. We stayed a year or two with my cousin Mike Kitzmann. Then my mother came after us. We lived for a while with her and her third husband, Mr. Meyer, near Le Sueur, Minnesota, until I was nearly of age. In 1881, I moved to Grand Forks County, North Dakota, and I have lived here ever since and am a progressive farmer.

Mrs. Krieger, the mother of John Lane, was shot by the Indian with a buckshot and was left for dead on the field. She was unconscious for a while, but revived and wandered for several days. She did not know where she was going. After shooting her, the Indians cut the clothes off her and lacerated her body in several places. Somewhere on the road she found a man's shirt and a buffalo robe. She put the shirt on and fastened the robe around her. She was wandering in a cornfield and was found by Mr. Thiele and Mr. Meyer. Mr. Thiele saw her long black hair and the red shirt and thought she was an Indian. He raised his gun to shoot her.

She turned around just then and he saw it was a white woman. He told me his heart stopped beating for a moment, he was so frightened because he came so near killing a white woman. They took her to the first house they came to and fixed her up some kind of bed and made her as comfortable as they could. The next day they turned her over to the soldiers at Birch Cooley. Here the Indians attacked the soldiers and the Battle of Birch Cooley was fought.[7]

It lasted two days and all that time Mrs. Krieger was lying in a wagon and received another bullet wound in her leg. After the battle she was taken to Fort Ridgely, where her wounds were dressed. While at the fort she learned that most of her children were alive and had been sent east to friends.

One of her little daughters (little Henrietta) had been taken prisoner. One of Mrs. Krieger's stepdaughters had picked up Mrs. Krieger's baby (she supposed that her stepmother was killed) and tried to care for it. She called to her aid August Urban, a thirteen-year-old boy, who had received a glance shot on the forehead. They picked up as many of the wounded as they could and took them to Krieger's house and did what they could for the sufferers. They stayed all night at the house and in the morning something frightened them. They ran out of the house and hid in the grass.

Mrs. Zabel, a woman who was wounded in the hip, advised them not to go back to the house again for the Indians were in the neighborhood and it was not safe to return.[8] They had left the baby asleep and several of the wounded children in the house and the Indians came back and finished their brutal work. They had gone out just in time.

The children then went back to Mr. Frass' house and found something to eat. Then they decided to go to Fort Ridgely. They took along some corn in a tin pail and ate as long as it lasted. They were on the road eleven days. The last day little five-year-old Minnie Krieger tired out completely. Mrs. Zabel advised the other children to leave her. But they would not forsake her. They took her to a creek and put water on her head and rested a while; then took her safely to the fort, which was only a few miles distant.

When they came within sight of the fort they were overjoyed for they knew their journey would soon be at an end. Mrs. Zabel thought it was a large Indian camp and did not want to go, but the children said they could see the soldiers. And the soldiers could see the children, also, and came to meet them and their trouble was ended. Mrs. Krieger afterwards married Mr. John Meyer, one of the men who found her in the cornfield.[9]

## *The Story of Mrs. Inefeld*

At the time of the outbreak we lived south of Middle Creek, not far from Beaver Creek. We had moved there in 1858 from New Ulm. Monday, August 18, 1862, my brother Mike Zitlaff, myself, and Lena Juni started off for the Lower Agency with butter and eggs, to trade at the store. We saw smoke and fire at the agency and asked Mr. Robinson, a half-breed who lived near the road, what it meant: if the Indians had broke[n] out.

He replied no, the Indians were hungry. If they took our cattle to let them have them; they would not harm us. We went back to our home. Lena Juni got out and went to her folks. They lived near us. As we were walking back we saw the Indians riding Mr. Henderson's white horses. My brother remarked that the Indians must have broken out or they would not have those horses.

When we got home my brother went to tell the neighbors what we had seen, and that we feared an outbreak was on. We started to load up a few articles and leave as quickly as possible. It took a little longer than we expected. While we were waiting for his return I left my baby with his sister, Mrs. Sieg, and ran to my own home to tell my husband what we had seen.[10]

While we were talking we saw Indians running to Mr. Hauf's house and heard shooting. My husband advised me to take the woods' road back to my sister's and not go on the prairie. He would stay in the woods awhile and watch and see if there was any truth in the report and that he would soon join me at my sister's. We waited at my sister's; my husband did not come. I went back to my house again to see what kept him. I found him dead on the floor, my furniture all thrown out of doors, my feather beds all ripped open and the feathers all scattered to the winds. I took one look at my husband and ran back to my sister's and took the prairie road. It was the nearest.

I told her what had happened and asked her for my baby. She handed it to me, but I did not know it, I was so excited. I told her it was not my child. She replied it was, so I took it. Just then Mr. Hauf came in and said the Indians had killed his wife.[11] His two little girls were visiting at my sister's. Then we all crowded into one wagon with a hayrack on and started to leave. The occupants of the load were my sister, Mrs. Meyer, and three children; Mr. And Mrs. Thiele and one child; Mr. Hauf and two children; my sister, Mrs. Sieg, and three children and her husband, Mr. Meyer and father; Mr. Zitlaff; my brother and his wife, Mary.

We had gone but a few yards when the Indians rose out of a corn field that we were passing, and fired on the crowd. Mr. Sieg called out, "Everybody jump from the wagon and scatter and save your lives as well as you can." We jumped. Mr. Hauf grabbed his two little girls and ran down the bluff ahead, while Mary, my brother's wife, and I followed him. While we were running an Indian shot Mr. Hauf and kicked his poor little girls to death.

I could not stand this and said, "O, Mary, let us go back and die where the rest are dying." We turned, and as we started an Indian raised his gun to shoot me. The cap snapped and the gun did not go off. He tried three different caps. Each one snapped. Then he put the gun down and took me by the hand and said, *wash ta* (good). I did not want to go. There were three squaws in the crowd. One took me by each hand and the other pushed from behind. The same Indian that tried to shoot me told Mary to sit down, while the squaws started off with me. I called back, "What is he doing with you, Mary?" She replied, "Nothing; he told me to sit down."

The next morning I heard a shot fired. I asked the squaws what it meant, and they told me that the Indians had killed a dog. The next day I asked for Mary and they told me that she was killed. The bodies of our friends were all found near the wagon. I never saw any of them again. Mr. Meyer and Mr. Thiele escaped and I was a prisoner. While I was in captivity, they used me quite well. The only troubles that I had was that my baby cried a good deal and the Indians often threatened to kill it.

One day I was sewing for the Indians when a young squaw tried to take my baby and kill it with a butcher knife. I grabbed and held it close to me. When she saw she could not get it, she struck me on the head. Her mother grabbed her by the shoulder and held her until she let me alone. I took care of my baby after that and did not sew for them again.

At first we had plenty to eat, but after awhile provisions got scarce and we did not fare so well. After the Battle of Wood Lake was fought, when the prisoners were all to be killed, a half-breed hid me behind some buffalo robes until we were released.

### *The Story of Minnie Krieger, Half-Sister of J. G. Lane, Age 6*

After the Indians surrounded the wagons, the men were killed first. My sister Lizzie told us all to jump from the wagon and throw ourselves face downward onto the ground, and lay still until she called us. When the Indians had gone, and she called, we arose among the dead and wounded. An awful thunderstorm came up; the rain was terrible. The wounded children were all crying.

My sisters, Lizzie, aged thirteen; Caroline, aged eleven; and Tillie, aged ten; picked up all the wounded children and carried them to my father's house, which was only a quarter of a mile away. The little ones were all partly helpless, and we could do nothing more for them. There were eighteen of them. After resting a little while, Caroline and Tillie went back to the dying women and men in the field and carried water to them. They stayed so long that Tillie got frightened and went with Mrs. Zabel to look for them, while I stayed with my little six-month-old sister. They all came home together. It was nearly morning. The shooting had occurred at four o'clock in the afternoon.

Mrs. Zabel was the only woman left alive. She was wounded in the hip and shoulder. Lizzie had taken off part of her clothing, washed the blood out of them, and dressed the wounds before morning. Mrs. Zabel said it was dangerous to stay at the house as the Indians might come back any moment and kill us. Most of the children were dead. We went to the brook and washed our faces, and then took the baby with us and went to another house to find something to eat. We found a little flour. Lizzie mixed it with water, fed the baby, and divided the balance, a few spoonfuls, among us.

The Indians had plundered all the houses. We left the baby to die, and although it broke Lizzie's heart, it could not be otherwise. We saw our mother lying dead as we supposed. But afterwards she was found wandering in a corn field, by Mr. Meyer, who later became her husband, my father having been killed.

We started at once on our journey to the fort. We wandered all day and came back at night to where we started. The Indians had come back, as Mrs. Zabel said they would, and had finished their fiendish work. They had burned the house and all the bodies we had carried there. We stayed in the woods all night, and in the morning went to where the people had been killed. The bodies were badly swollen and had turned black. We shed a few tears and started the second time to find the fort.

At first we traveled by day, but had to give that up, as we came near being captured several times. So we slept during the day and traveled at night. We had nothing to eat and were obliged to chew grass and drink water. One day we stopped under a big tree surrounded by a lot of brush. Not far off was a house and garden. Lizzie went to see if she could find anything to eat. The only thing that she could find was some large, red unions, and she returned with them. We knelt down and said our prayers and then began to eat our onions. The tears were running down our cheeks, so strong were the onions.

This was too much for Lizzie. She threw herself onto the ground, hid her face and cried as if her heart would break. When she got through crying, we started our perilous night journey. It was dusk one evening when we came to about fifteen bodies of men, women, and children lying in all directions. We also saw many bodies while we traveled by daylight. We were nearly caught again near the place where the dead people were. There were a lot of Indians coming on foot and we were so close to them it is a wonder that they did not see us. We were sitting in the brush and kept perfectly still until they passed and then resumed our journey.

There was one awful dark night, when we were about five miles from the fort. We could see nothing. Suddenly right in the road ahead of us came a lot of Indians. We all stepped out of the road and laid down in the grass until they passed us. That same night we must have been within a few rods of my two brothers, J. G. Lane and Gottlieb, and August Guess. So we found afterwards. We concluded not to travel any more that night.

In the morning we almost ran into an Indian camp. They never noticed us and we ran back and hid in the woods. We were so tired. I do not know how long we traveled. At last we came within sight of the fort. We sat down and rested. It seemed enough for us to look at it. The soldiers saw us through their field glasses and sent a team to meet us.

When we got to the fort we found out that our brothers, John G. Lane and Gottlieb, were alive and had gotten to the fort ahead of us. The last day I played out completely and could go no farther. Mrs. Zabel told Lizzie to leave me to die, but she dragged me to the brook and bathed my face and said she would stay with me. I never forgave Mrs. Zabel. Poor Lizzie never was strong after that awful trip of twenty-seven miles that we made in twelve days. She was never rewarded for her kindness on earth. May she reap her reward in Heaven.[12]

# Editor's Conclusion

*I*S THERE AN AWARENESS TODAY that August 1862 is second only in American history to the tragedy of 9-11? Probably not, and there are several reasons.

First of all, it was a tragedy within the tragedy of the Civil War. The nation simply was overwhelmed by the war. In the very same month of August 1862, Union forces had suffered a severe blow with the defeat at the Second Battle of Bull Run, resulting in the loss of eight hundred soldiers. The nation's attention was riveted on the Civil War, not on what was happening on the Minnesota frontier, even though the death toll there equaled that of the Second Battle of Bull Run.[1] And, the war would continue for several more years, resulting in even greater casualties.

A second reason was that the death and destruction of the uprising surpassed human comprehension—nothing like this ever had happened on such a phenomenal scale. Jane Grey Swisshelm commented during her speaking tour in the East that everyone "totally disbelieves the story of the outrages committed."[2] People simply could not believe, or fathom, the horrific stories.

Also, few today are aware of the huge death toll, and of what actually happened. Although some may ascribe the death toll suffered by a civilian population, as well as the atrocities, as the kind of "collateral damage" attendant to warfare, it should be noted that these have clearly now been designated as crimes against humanity by the rulings of international agreements, such as the Geneva Conventions.

A third reason was that many families were recently arrived immigrants without other contacts elsewhere in the country, and their stories did not get told beyond the confines of their own immediate communities, and only later did some of them find their way into local and regional histories.

Also, "often it was impossible to extract facts from the refugees. Many settlers could speak little English even when calm; now they had seen mates beheaded or children nailed to cabin doors, and were wildly excited. No doubt they had stories to tell; too bad they were so incoherent."[3]

Finally, as has been mentioned before, all of this took place in an age before the media of today. "No press associations had correspondents in or near Sioux country. Pictorial journalism had not been invented; only a few photographers even experimented with cameras on Civil War battlefields."[4] The sneak attack of 9-11 received round-the-clock coverage, but there was no such coverage in 1862. If something like August 1862 would happen today with eight hundred deaths, there is no question that it would become a media event of international proportions with round-the-clock coverage.

In spite of the general unawareness today of what happened then, the impact of the uprising was great. Not only did it abruptly change the history of the region, "but it grossly affected the course of the state's progress, and had its bearing nationally, also."[5] And in the long run, its impact was more than merely an uprising, as it changed the region forever.

The Renville County history alone lists almost seventy families that were either completely or partly wiped out as a result of the uprising. It claimed that county soil was sanctified "by the blood of martyrs," and that "it is fitting that many hallowed spots, here and there, should be marked with permanent marble and granite, suitably inscribed as a memorial to the past and an inspiration to the future."[6]

One such monument, the Schwandt Monument, was erected August 18, 1915, near the spot where seven people were killed on August 18, 1862. The monument bears the names of those who lost their lives: Johann and Christina Schwandt and their children, Frederick and Christian, John Walz, Karolina Schwandt Walz, and John Frass.[7]

The monument was dedicated in 1915 during the First World War. Dr. Warren Upham from the Minnesota State Historical Society sought a meaning to it all in his remarks, stating that in dedicating the monument telling of the hatred and massacre "which befell a German family of pioneers here . . . let us not forget the bright flower of a lifelong friendship which blossomed above the graves, gladdening the life of a rescued survivor of that family and the life of the kind Dakota woman, Snahnah, her rescuer."

Upham noted that the story of Schwandt and Snahnah had been published, and that they were children of peoples "who met in mortal conflict, the one a captive German girl and the other a bereaved Dakota mother. They loved each other with affection that may be likened to that of David and Jonathan three thousand years ago."

And in his closing remarks, he asked those present, as well as future generations: "Can we learn something from this—does it even shed forth a ray of hope that . . . may be the beginning of trust and helpfulness, of mutual respect and friendship?"

Aside from this ray of hope emanating from this noteworthy example of humanity, another contribution was the exemplary service performed by Schwandt and Busse, who documented and recorded not only their experiences, but those of their neighbors, thereby providing insight into the tragic fate of eight hundred innocent men, women, and children who perished in 1862.

*This monument is located in Flora Township in memory of the families killed there in August 1862. In sections 33–35 of the township, thirty-nine people were killed, including members of the Schwandt, Busse, and Kochendorfer families. The death toll here for a township was second only to Milford, just west of New Ulm, where fifty-one were killed.*

# Notes

**Preface**

1. For a list of the works by the editor on the topic, see the Sources.
2. See Mary Schwandt-Schmidt, "The Story of Mary Schwandt," *Minnesota Historical Society Collections* 6 (1894): 461–474, and Minnie Buce Carrigan, *Captured by the Indians: Reminiscences of Pioneer Life in Minnesota* (Buffalo Lake, Minnesota: *The News Print*, 1912). Regarding the spelling of the latter's name, note that Wilhelmina Busse used the shortened form of her first name "Minnie," her married name was Carrigan, and that she apparently felt that "Buce" approximated the pronunciation of the German name "Busse." In the 1970s, the Garland Publishing Co., New York, published the *Garland Library of Narratives of North American Indian Captivities*, which consisted of personal accounts and narratives. Of the approximately 290 titles, only eight were by, or about German Americans, including the narratives by Schwandt and Busse. Of those eight, five pertained to the eighteenth century, and one to the early nineteenth century.
3. According to Kenneth Carley, the settlers in Renville and neighboring Brown County, "the two areas where the loss of life was the greatest—were largely Germans. They had lived on friendly terms with the Dakota, whom they knew as wandering, usually hungry, beggars, and at first they could not believe that the Indians were bent on anything as serious as murder." See Carley's *The Sioux Uprising of 1862*, 2d ed. (St. Paul: Minnesota Historical Society, 1976), 21.
4. The Jacob Nix edition appeared as *The Sioux Uprising in Minnesota, 1862: Jacob Nix's Eyewitness History. German/English Edition* (Indianapolis: Max Kade German-American Center & Indiana German Heritage Society, 1994).
5. According to the recent history of Renville County, "Flora Township is located in a very historical part of Renville County. The Schwandt Memorial was erected August 18, 1915, on section 33, in memory of the Schwandt family who were killed by the Indians on August 18, 1862. Another monument is located south of the Middle Creek Church in memory of families in that area killed during the Sioux uprising." Regarding the nearby church, the history notes, "On August 18, 1862, Rev. Seder preached to a congregation of over

100 people and a little after noon the following day was killed, along with 75 others of the congregation, in the Sioux uprising. A man by the name of Louis Thiele was the only one of those who escaped that came back to live in the community." See *Renville County History Book 1980* (Dallas, Texas: Taylor Publishing Co., 1981), 299. Regarding my great-grandparents, grandfather, and the Tolzmann farm, see Nix, *The Sioux Uprising in Minnesota, 1862,* xvii–xviii. My great-grandfather, Carl Tolzmann, who had emigrated from Pomerania in 1855, moved with family to Renville County to the farm on section 33 of Flora Township, so as to be located adjacent to that of his wife's parents, the Christian Sperber family, whose farm was located on section 34. See Franklyn Curtiss-Wedge, ed., 2 vols., *The History of Renville County, Minnesota* (Chicago: H. C. Cooper Jr., & Co., 1916), 2:1314 (hereafter referred to as Curtiss-Wedge, *Renville County*). At that time, many settlers were moving to Renville County, which was almost entirely depopulated as a result of the uprising. Today, residents in Flora Township, Renville County, in and around the Tolzmann farm, are well aware of what happened there in 1862, as well as to my grandfather, which is an indication of the living presence that past history has.

## Introduction

1. Gary Clayton Anderson and Alan R. Woolworth, eds., *Through Dakota Eyes: Narrative Accounts of the Minnesota Indian War of 1862* (St. Paul: Minnesota Historical Society, 1988), 1.
2. Documentation on the casualties can be found in Marion P. Satterlee., *Outbreak and Massacre by the Dakota Indians in Minnesota in 1862: Marion P. Satterlee's Minute Account of the Outbreak, with Exact Locations, Names of All Victims, Prisoners at Camp Release, Refugees at Fort Ridgely, etc. Complete List of Indians Killed in Battle and Those Hung, and Those Pardoned at Rock Island, Iowa*, ed. Don Heinrich Tolzmann (Bowie, Maryland: Heritage Books, Inc., 2001) (hereafter cited as Satterlee, *Account*). In addition, more casualties can be found listed in the histories for Brown and Renville counties. References to the county histories can be found listed with the sources on page 93. Actually, we never will know the exact number of those killed due to the fact that people were killed working in the field, along roadsides, near rivers and creeks, etc., and that not everyone was accounted for, or ever located. On this point, C. M. Oehler comments: "Tallies of casualties could not be kept during the killings. Settlers who paused in flight to bury murdered neighbors might themselves be slain before they reported the burials. A count of graves could not determine the number of casualties. Except by disinterment, it could not be known how many bodies each mound covered. Some graves were not found, and never would be. Some victims were not buried; wind and rain erased the remains of some who perished in flames of lonely cabins. Those who died in swamps, thickets, or deep prairie grass would never be known." Jane Grey Swisshelm, a pioneer newspaper editor, estimated the death toll at fifteen hundred, while the St. Peter *Tribune* thought the number to be as high

as two thousand, stating that "doubtless hundreds have been slain and left upon the surface will never be found, as decomposition is nearly complete, and the prairie fires now ravaging the whole upper country will consume what may yet remain." Indian agent Thomas Galbraith took a census of the missing area by area, and came up with a death toll of 737, but stated there were many others he could not establish for sure. However, President Lincoln placed the number at eight hundred, and based on the resources at his disposal, and his estimate has stood the test of time. See C. M. Oehler, *The Great Sioux Uprising* (New York: Oxford University Press, 1959), 234–35.
3. Of the many works written about the uprising, the following are especially useful: Minnesota Board of Commissioners on Publication of History of Minnesota in Civil and Indian Wars, *Minnesota in the Civil and Indian Wars, 1861–65*, 2d ed., (St. Paul: The Board, 1891); William Watts Folwell, *A History of Minnesota*, rev. ed., 4 vols. (St. Paul: Minnesota Historical Society, 1956–69); and Carley, *The Sioux Uprising of 1862*. For a more recent survey, see *The War for the Plains* (Alexandria, Virginia: Time Life, Inc., 1994), especially 6–61.
4. According to Charles E. Flandrau, the 1862 uprising surpasses all other frontier conflicts "when viewed in the light of the number of settlers and others massacred, the amount of property destroyed, and the horrible atrocities" that were committed. See *Minnesota in the Civil and Indian Wars, 1861–65*, 753.
5. The population statistics on the Sioux are from Anderson and Woolworth, *Through Dakota Eyes*, 8. For the history of Brown and Renville counties, see the county histories listed in the sources on page 93. For the history of Redwood County, see Franklyn Curtiss-Wedge, *The History of Redwood County, Minnesota* (Chicago: H. C. Cooper Jr. & Co., 1916). For a more recent history of the latter, see Wayne E. Webb and Jasper Swedberg, *Redwood, the Story of a County*, (Redwood Falls, Minnesota: Redwood County Board of Commissioners, 1964).
6. Curtiss-Wedge, *Renville County*.
7. Louis A. Fritsche, ed., *History of Brown County, Minnesota*, 2 vols. (Indianapolis: B. F. Bowen & Co., 1916).
8. Curtiss-Wedge, *Renville County*, 1:50.
9. Ibid., 2:1313.
10. Anderson and Woolworth, *Through Dakota Eyes*, 3.
11. Marion P. Satterlee, ed., addenda to *The Court Proceedings in the Trial of Dakota Indians Following the Massacre in Minnesota in August 1862* (Minneapolis: Marion P. Satterlee, 1927), 17–19. Ignatius Donnelly, lieutenant governor of Minnesota, characterized the Sunday afternoon murder of five persons as an "accidental outrage," which "fell like a spark of fire, on mass of discontent, long accumulated and ready for it." See Flora Warren Seymour, *Indian Agents of the Old Frontier* (New York: Appelton-Century, 1941), 29.
12. In 1857, Inkpaduta (Scarlet Point) led a group of renegade Lower Sioux to Lake Okoboji, Iowa, where they killed more than thirty persons, and then went to Jackson County, Minnesota, where they killed several more persons. Inkpaduta escaped to the Dakota Territory, and the Indian office in Washington,

D.C., then notified the Minnesota Sioux that they would be held accountable for them, and that no annuities would be turned over until he was found. Little Crow led a futile search for him, and then the Indian office dropped its conditions on the matter. See Carley, *The Sioux Uprising*, 5. See also L. P. Lee, *History of the Spirit Lake Massacre! 8th March, 1857, and of Miss Abigail Gardner's Three Month's Captivity Among the Indians. According to Her Own Account, As Given to L. P. Lee.* (New Britain, Conn.: L. P. Lee, 1857); and Mary Hawker Bakeman, ed., *Legends, Letters, and Lies: Readings on the Spirit Lake Massacre of 1857* (Roseville, MN: Genealogical Books, 2001). The Inkpaduta incident appears as a sign of things to come, and should have alerted officials that the current state of affairs was awry, and in need of attention. The same pattern of events re-occurred in 1862 with attacks on civilians, captivities, etc., and then the guilty parties escaping to the Dakota Territory.

13. Thomas J. Galbraith, who held the honorary title of major, was the government Indian agent, who arrived in 1861 and lived at the Upper Agency. He was a political appointment, who "knew nothing about Indians. In addition, he lacked the commitment or dedication to fair treatment for the Indians that some of his predecessors had demonstrated." See Duane Schultz, *Over the Earth I Come: The Great Sioux Uprising of 1862* (New York: St. Martin's Press, 1992), 11. See also Seymour, *Indian Agents of the Old Frontier*, 26–34. Galbraith, obviously, was the wrong person in the wrong place at the wrong time. Andrew Myrick was a trader who owned stores at both the Lower and Upper Agencies, and would pay for the remarks he made. See Gary Clayton Anderson, "Myrick's Insult: A Fresh Look at Myth and Reality," *Minnesota History*. 48:5 (1983): 198–206, and also his *Kinsmen of Another Kind: Dakota-White Relations in the Upper Mississippi Valley, 1650–1862* (Lincoln: University of Nebraska Press, 1984).

14. See note 13 regarding Myrick.

15. Regarding Little Crow and other Sioux leaders, see Gary Clayton Anderson, *Little Crow, Spokesman for the Sioux* (St. Paul: Minnesota Historical Society, 1986) and *War for the Plains*, 34–38, 59. Lincoln's decision was that those guilty of murder and rape should be executed. In making the decision, he distinguished between involvement in battles and massacre, the latter of which was categorized as murder. His decision on the cases was issued on December 6, 1862, and he explained his rationale to the U.S. Senate as follows: "Anxious to not act with so much clemency as to encourage another outbreak on the one hand, nor with so much severity to be real cruelty on the other, I caused a careful examination of the record of trials to be made, in view of first ordering the execution of such as had been proved guilty of violating females. Contrary to my expectations, only two of this class were found. I then directed a further examination, and a classification of all who were proved to have participated in massacres, as distinguished from participation in battles." See Daniel W. Homstad, "Lincoln's Agonizing Decision," *American History*, 36:5 (2001): 36. See also Schultz, *Over the Earth I Come*, 243–64. Lincoln's decision presages that of the Geneva Conventions, which state: "Parties of a conflict shall at all times

distinguish between the civilian population and combatants in order to spare civilian population and property. Neither the civilian population as such nor civilian persons shall be the object of attack. Attacks shall be directed solely against military objectives." See *Basic Rules of the Geneva Conventions and Their Additional Protocols.* (Geneva: ICRC, 1983).

## Chapter 1, The Story of Mary Schwandt

1. Schwandt's memoir contains a note signed with the initials W. R. M. as follows: "I remember Mary Schwandt at Camp Release, Sept. 26, 1862, when she, with other captives, was surrendered after the Battle of Wood Lake. I was a member of the military commission before whom were tried the 306 Sioux, convicted of taking part in the outbreak (38 of whom were executed at Mankato; the others [were] kept prisoners at Rock Island until after the close of the Civil War). Mary Schwandt, then a girl of sixteen, testified against the prisoners, relating the same facts substantially given in this narrative." The initials were those of Col. Wm. R. Marshall, a member of the Military Commission created by General Sibley's Order No. 55, Sept. 26, 1862. Col. Marshall had served with the Sixth Regiment, Minnesota Volunteers Company, during the uprising. See Satterlee, *The Court Proceedings,* 1. Schwandt's story, therefore, was being published with an official stamp of approval by a member of the Commission, which had taken her testimony after the uprising. This is not the only account by Schwandt. In 1864, Charles S. Bryant published a history of the uprising with several personal accounts, including an account by Schwandt that was brief, but more graphic with regard to her experiences. See Charles S. Bryant, *A History of the Great Massacre by the Sioux Indians in Minnesota, Including the Personal Narratives of Many Who Escaped* (Cincinnati: Rickey & Carroll, 1864).
2. The name of the creek was actually Middle Creek, and Sacred Heart Township was adjacent to Flora Township. However, it should be noted that the townships were not drawn up until after the uprising, so that such names did not apply when the Schwandts lived there. The immigration of the Schwandt family was part of the great wave of German immigration that took place in the 1850s. See Don Heinrich Tolzmann, *The German-American Experience.* (Amherst, NY: Humanity Books, 2000), 151–208.
3. Flora Township was across the Minnesota River from Shakopee's village and as Schwandt observes, the Indians frequented the area, requesting food.
4. Schwandt here refers to a latter day visit to the farm during which she became acquainted with the Tolzmann family.
5. New Ulm is located about forty miles from the Flora Township farm.
6. Godfrey occupies an interesting and controversial place in the history of the uprising. Joseph Godfrey was the son of a Frenchman and a mulatto woman, was married to a Sioux woman, and had lived with the Indians for about five years. He was charged with murder based on the testimony of Schwandt and

others. However, they could not swear to having seen him kill anyone, only to having seen him in war paint and dressed as a member of war parties, and that they had heard of him bragging of killing at least seven people, and appeared supportive of the killing that took place. However, in exchange for his testimony as the chief witness in the trial against the Indians, Godfrey's sentence was commuted to ten years, and he was pardoned in 1866 at Rock Island, Iowa. Many, however, considered Godfrey "the devil incarnate," according to Satterlee. See Satterlee, *Account*, 39. An indication is provided of this viewpoint by Nix, who writes that Godfrey was "the cruelest of the cruel red murder gang. Hair-raising stories of deeds of cruelty were reported of this monster. But now captured, the cowardly brute trembled at the thought of a twenty-fold deserved death. In order to save his miserable life he appeared as a state witness against his own accomplices, against men of the tribe to which he had belonged for years . . . (he) showed himself as a splendid witness, for he brought things to the point that thirty-eight of his shameful accomplices were sentenced to death and a number of others sent to the penitentiary." See Don Heinrich Tolzmann, ed., *The Sioux Uprising in Minnesota, 1862: Jacob Nix's Eyewitness History*, 130.

7. According to Schultz, "the death greatly affected the fourteen-year-old Schwandt. She had been raped and she knew she could be killed at any time. She kept her spirits from flagging with the hope that one day the terror would end and she would be reunited with her family. That hope was dashed on the same day her friend died." See Schultz, *Over the Earth I Come*, 133. In her 1864 account, which was not included in the 1894 account, Schwandt writes of what happened to her after she was brought to the camp of Wacouta, chief of the Wapekuta tribe: "After awhile a number (of the tribe) came, and, after annoying me with their loathsome attentions for a long time, one of them laid his hands forcibly upon me, when I screamed, and one of the fiends struck me on my mouth with his hand, causing the blood to flow very freely. They then took me out by force, to an unoccupied teepee, near the house, and perpetrated the most horrible and nameless outrages upon my person. These outrages were repeated, at different times during my captivity." Charles S. Bryant then comments in an editorial note that "the details of this poor girl's awful treatment, in our possession, are too revolting for publication." See Bryant, *History of the Great Massacre*, 339–40.

8. Snana was "a beautiful Sioux woman of twenty-three. . . . She was unusually well educated, having attended the Reverend Williamson's mission school in her childhood. She spoke English fluently and was rarely without her Bible." She and her husband, Good Thunder, were married in the Episcopal Church, were farmer Indians, and were both opposed to the uprising. See Schultz, *Over the Earth I Come*, 171. After learning of the publication of the account of Mary Schwandt, Snana visited Schwandt for the first time in thirty-two years, in 1894, in St. Paul, Minnesota. She wrote that "it was just as if I went to visit my own child." She wrote of her early life and "then came the dreadful outbreak of

1862. About eight days before the massacre, my oldest daughter had died, and hence my heart was still aching when the outbreak occurred. Two of my uncles went out to see the outbreak, and I told them that if they should happen to see any girl I wished them not to hurt her but bring her to me that I might keep her for a length of time. One evening one of my uncles came to me and said that he had not found any girl, but that there was a young man who brought a nice looking girl. I asked my mother to go and bring this girl to me; and my uncle, having heard of our conversation, advised my mother that she ought to take something along with her in order to buy this girl. Hence I told her to take my pony with her, which she did." She continues that "when she brought me this girl, whose name was Mary Schwandt, she was much larger than the one I had lost, who was only seven years old; but my heart was so sad that I was willing to take any girl at that time. The reason why I wished to keep this girl was to have her in place of the one I lost. So I loved her and pitied her, and she was dear to me just the same as my own daughter." She also comments on how she protected Mary Schwandt noting that "during the outbreak, when some of the Indians got killed, they began to kill the captives. At such times I always hid my dear captive white girl. At one time the Indians reported that one of the captives was shot down, and also that another one, at Shakopee's camp, had her throat cut; and I thought to myself that if they would kill my girl they must kill me first. Though I had two of my own children at that time with me, I thought of this girl just as much as of the others." See Snana, "Narration of A Friendly Sioux," *Minnesota Historical Society Collections.* 9 (1901): 426–30.

9. Schwandt here refers to the Battle of Wood Lake, which took place on September 22–23, 1862. This battle essentially brought the uprising to an end. "Knowing that Sibley with his command had started out to capture them, the hostiles resolved to make a desperate effort to stop them. After a very heated council, it was decided to creep on the camp and ambush the command as it started under way in the early morning. A squad from the Third Regiment started with teams to get some potatoes at a nearby point and, driving across the prairie, ran into the concealed warriors. The fight was on at once, and the ambush defeated. In about two hours they were well whipped, and Little Crow and most of the hostiles were heading for the wild west, never to annoy Minnesota, in numbers, again." See Satterlee, *Account,* 71.

10. Sarah F. Wakefield, like Godfrey, is another controversial figure in the history of the uprising, and was shunned by the Indians and settlers alike. She testified on behalf of Chaska, who was mistakenly hung for Chaskadon, who had killed a pregnant woman and cut out her child, so that he was hung for a crime of which he was not guilty, whereas the guilty party escaped punishment. However, Chaska was guilty for another crime as an accessory to the murder of George Gleason, a clerk of the agent Galbraith, but was not tried for this due to the mistaken identity. After his execution, Wakefield tried to defend Chaska, claiming that Chaska had protected her during her six weeks of captivity, but it was suspected that she had slept with him, and that she preferred living with

him to her own husband, Dr. Wakefield. The trial judges had also been suspicious of her, and there is no question where Schwandt stood with respect to Wakefield. See Sarah W. Wakefield, *Six Weeks in the Sioux Teepees (Little Crow's Camp): A Narrative of Indian Captivity* (Shakopee, Minnesota: Argus, 1864. With regard to the execution, Oehler comments: "Most of the war's instigators, and most of the perpetrators of civilian massacres, were not on the list of those to be hung for the reason that they had not waited to surrender. . . . Probably less than one in twenty, and certainly not more than one-tenth, of the rapists and murderers that Sibley had been sent to capture were on the list." Also when the Indians were finally sent to the Dakota reservation, there were only 1,700, whereas the reservation had had a population of 6,000. Therefore, many of the culprits had escaped and the rest simply scattered either to Canada or to Dakota Territory. See Oehler, *The Great Sioux Uprising*, 219.

11. Details as to what was found at the Schwandt home are provided by the Rev. Alexander Berghold: "Schwandt's son-in-law was lying on the door steps with three bullets in his body. His wife (Schwandt's daughter), who had been with child, was found dead, her womb cut open and the unborn child nailed to a tree. Her brother, a thirteen-year-old lad, whom the Indians thought they had killed, saw how the child was taken alive from the womb of his sister, and nailed to the tree, where it lived for a little while. This terrible deed was done in the forenoon of August the 18th. The mother was found in the field beheaded. Beside her lay the body of their hired man, Frass. Towards evening the boy regained a little strength and fled into the settlement, a distance of three miles. He entered Bushe's house only to find some thirty corpses, and among them a three-year-old child, wounded, and sitting beside its dead mother. The boy took the child with him, carried it about four miles, and being unable to take it farther, left it at a house, promising to return the next morning. He did this in order to be able to save himself. He made good his escape to Fort Ridgely, traveling for four nights, and hiding the day. The child was afterwards found in captivity among the Indians, and was brought to Fort Ridgely, where it died from the effects of the wounds and exposure." It should be noted that Mrs. Schwandt's torso was found in the woods near the home, but her head was never found. Also, if it had not been for the survival of Mary Schwandt's brother, August, some of these details would remain unknown, which highlights the importance of the reports and narratives of survivors. See Alexander Berghold, *The Indian's Revenge: Or, Days of Horror: Some Appalling Events in the History of the Sioux* (San Francisco, California: P. J. Thomas, 1891), 164–65. Satterlee writes of sections 33–35 in Flora Township that they "were veritable slaughter fields, thirty-nine people being killed there." See Satterlee, *Account*, 27. Schultz writes in relation to the Schwandt family that: "scores of families met deaths in similar ways, many of them trapped in houses that were set on fire. Women and girls endured multiple rapes before being stabbed to death. Children were nailed to doors; heads, hands, and feet chopped off; bodies mutilated in the most appalling ways. Many of these atrocities were traditional ways of killing among the Sioux . . . . Limbs and heads were severed so that enemies would be at a disad-

vantage if the Sioux encountered them in the hereafter. They believed that a person who died without a head or hands entered the next world in that condition and remained so for all eternity." See Schultz, *Over the Earth I Come*, 60. Oehler notes that often "the callers greeted their hosts as old friends warmly with everyone, and kissed some as a token of special esteem." And, "then the visitors split the hosts' skull, clubbed their children to death, raped daughters, hacked heads from the dead, slashed breasts from the corpses of women and genitals from the bodies of men, took what food and furnishings they could carry, cut, chopped, or smashed the rest, and set fire to the ruins before leaving for the next cabin." Deception and surprise were, therefore, a key part of the plan of attack on the settlers who were mostly unarmed, as "few of the newcomers were seasoned frontiersmen, and few had guns. They had come to farm rather than hunt. They were on prairie land and not deer country, and such guns as they had were shot-guns instead of rifles. Especially in the recently opened areas, many immigrants would not have known how to shoot a weapon if they had owned one." See Oehler, *The Great Sioux Uprising*, 49.

12. Given the experiences of Schwandt, the reference to the civilization process can be understood in historical context.

## Chapter 2, The Story of Wilhelmina Busse

[*Note: In Busse's work, errors and inconsistencies in the spelling of family names have been corrected whenever the correct form could be verified. For example, Busse's own name has several variants, but the correct German spelling is "Busse." In some cases, the author Anglicizes a name, such as Smith for Schmidt. In other cases, she misspells names, such as Krus for Krause, or Kitzman for Kitzmann, or Kochendurfer for Kochendorfer. The editor verified spellings against local histories, and also consulted his father, Eckhart Tolzmann, born 1904 in Renville County.*]

1. The area discussed by the author referred to as "the theater in which was staged one of the greatest tragedies the nation has ever seen," provides some insight into the kind of impact the uprising had. For a general survey of the uprising in Renville County in particular, see Curtiss-Wedge, *Renville County*, especially vol. 2.

2. The feeling was widespread that the uprising would not have occurred without the Civil War, with troops involved elsewhere. Wilhelm Kaufmann's history of the Civil War observes that the Sioux "exploited the time in which all men capable of fighting in the German settlement of New Ulm, Minnesota, and environs were in the field fighting for the Union, and they fell on undefended settlers." See Wilhelm Kaufmann, *The Germans in the American Civil War: With a Biographical Directory,* trans. Steven Rowan, ed. Don Heinrich Tolzmann. (Carlisle, Pa.: John Kallmann, 1999), 343.

3. Many Germans who came to Minnesota first stopped in Wisconsin, and then proceeded on to Minnesota. See, for example, the biographies of immigrants in L. A. Fritsche, ed., *Brown County (New Ulm), Minnesota Pioneers and Their Families. Excerpted from History of Brown County, Minnesota: Its People, Industries and Institutions. With an Introduction by Don Heinrich Tolzmann.* (Baltimore, MD: Clearfield Co., Inc., 2001).
4. According to Satterlee, Augusta Lenz, daughter of Ernest Lenz, captured at Middle Creek, was surrendered at Camp Release. See Satterlee, *Account*, 92.
5. Regarding the Kitzmann family at Middle Creek: "Paul, wife, infant Paul, Pauline, and Wilhelmina, killed. Captured: Louis and Gustaf. The latter, a child of three years, was cut to pieces by Indians because he cried so much." See Satterlee, *Account*, 32.
6. Schwandt also notes that the Indians were frequent visitors from across the Minnesota River.
7. Schwandt comments also on the money that her family had brought to America, thus reminding us that the mid-nineteenth century immigrants were making an investment in the future by coming to the U.S.
8. The question commonly arises as to the origin of the name "Sacred Heart." According to the Renville County history, there are two versions to the story: "One story concerns Charles Patterson, who settled in Flora Township, on the Renville County side of the rapids of the Minnesota River, in 1783, and there established a trading post. He wore a peculiar shaped hat, made of fur, and the Indians began to call him the man with the strange or mysterious or magic hat. Their word 'wakan,' really meaning 'spirit,' being applied to anything that they did not quite comprehend or that was unusual in any way. Each particular clan of Indians had some animal which they never killed and which they regarded as sacred. It has been said that the Indian then living in this locality esteemed the bear sacred and that Patterson's hat was made of the fur from a great bear which had frequented the neighborhood. Gradually they began to refer to the man himself as 'the Spirit Hat" or 'the sacred hat,' the meaning being the same as the name form which 'medicine hat' was translated. Later the white people corrupted the name of 'Sacred Hat' to Sacred Heart. A much more pleasing story of the name was told to Ed. O'Connor of Sacred Heart, by Louis G. Brisbois, a French pioneer of Hawk Creek Township. He declared that in the early days, the mouth of the Sacred Heart creek formed in the shape of a heart and that a missionary-priest, inspired by this, had given the name of Sacred Heart to a mission of French half-breeds and Indians that he had established here, and that the locality gradually took the name of this early mission, still retaining it long after the mission had passed into oblivion." See Curtiss-Wedge, *Renville County,* 2:1332.
9. The Schwandt family arrived in Minnesota only a few months before the uprising in August 1862.

10. Regarding the Mannweiler family at Middle Creek, Gottlieb Mannweiler "was a son-in-law of Ernest Lenz. He was making ready to go, when Indians appeared and he was killed. His wife, and sister, Augusta Lenz, were approaching, from the Lenz home, and just came in sight. They turned and ran back, but Augusta was overtaken and captured. Mannweiler was superintendent of the Middle Creek Sunday school." See Satterlee, *Account*, 31.
11. Thiele lived in the Middle Creek settlement. See note 12 regarding his family.
12. Regarding Zitlaff and Inefeld, on section 7 (Middle Creek), lived John Zitlaff, a widower, with his son and wife Mary (nee Juni), and near them three sons-in-law, John J. Meyer, William Inefeld, and John Sieg, also Louis Thiele. On their way to the Agency, Michael Zitlaff, Mrs. Inefeld, and Lena Juni near Bear Creek, saw some Indian with Henderson's team, and heard much shooting at the Agency. Apprehending trouble, Zitlaff turned back; Lena Juni went to her parents. Mrs. Inefeld told her husband of the circumstances, and he sent her to Meyer's saying he would follow. She went back to see what kept him and found him dead on the floor. She ran back to Meyer's where all were waiting to start. There were in the party: John Zitlaff; Michael Zitlaff and wife; Mrs. Inefeld and child; John Sieg, wife and three children; John J. Meyer, wife and three children; Ernest Hauf and his two little girls, who had come from some little distance to the west; (his wife and two other children had been murdered at the home); and Louis Thiele, wife and child." See Satterlee, *Account*, 26–27.
13. Reverend Seder was a guest at the home of John Lettou at the Middle Creek settlement, and he "conducted services alternately at the Middle Creek and Sacred Heart settlements on Sundays, for the German Evangelical Church, and the gathering at Lettou's the 17th had been a large one. Word of the trouble came, and he remained to aid in the preparations for flight. When leaving, he led the way, but a short distance off was shot and killed; Lettou and a small son were killed, but the mother and four children escaped to Fort Ridgely." See Satterlee, *Account*, 30.
14. John Roessler and his wife (of Middle Creek) were grinding a scythe when the Indians approached and killed both of them, while "two children were killed and thrown on as ash pile. Frederick Roessler, probably related, was killed, but no record but that of the Evangelical Church, a mere statement is found." See Sattterlee, *Account*, 28.
15. Regarding the Boelter family, the family consisted of the families of two brothers, Michael and John Boelter, as well as the parents, Gottlieb and his wife. On the way home, Michael "found his mother and his three children murdered and mutilated, at the house. On calling to the field where his wife, father, and brother had been at work, he was answered by Indian yells, and beat a hasty retreat. These three were killed in the field, and it is likely that John Boelter is the man who bit the thumb of Cut Nose nearly off in a death struggle. Michael had warned John's wife, Justina, of danger, and running to the house, he picked up the baby boy Julius, and told Justina to follow him. She took the other two

children and started, but hearing the Indians coming, hid in the underbrush and they passed by her. For nearly nine weeks they stayed in this hiding place living on herbs and some raw vegetables from the field. One of the children, Emilia, died from exposure and hunger, in the fourth week. The poor woman was terribly frightened by the shooting about her; first by Indians then by the searching parties; she undoubtedly heard the battle at Birch Coulie, and for serveral days the hostile camp was just across the Minnesota River. She finally resolved to die in her own home and managed to reach it with the remaining child, and was there when discovered by two soldiers of a searching party. This on Monday, just nine weeks from the day she left it. The condition of the woman and the child was so pitiful that the soldiers were moved to tears. Her history is remarkable." See Satterlee, *Account*, 29.

16. Regarding Justine Boelter, see the previous note. See also Berghold, *The Indians' Revenge*, 179.
17. Regarding Kochendorfer, "The home of John Kochendorfer (Middle Creek settlement), some eighty rods away (from the Schwandt home), was attacked and Kochdorfer was shot down in the doorway and the baby Sarah and the wife, in the house. The father lived long enough to direct his other children to hide in the brush; they escaped to the fort, aided by Michael Boelter and the Ernest Lenz family." See Satterlee, *Account*, 28.
18. The hymn text: How tedious and gloomy the hours, when Jesus is no longer here, even the flowers, the birds, and joy, lose all their beauty to me!
19. Regarding Mrs. Urban and her five children: They were from the Sacred Heart Settlement, and were surrendered at Camp Release. See Satterlee, *Account*, 93.
20. Ludwig Kitzmann, age fourteen, son of Paul, captured at Sacred Heart, was surrendered at Camp Release. See Satterlee, *Account*, 91.
21. Regarding Henrietta Krieger, "Krieger Family—Killed, Frederick, and infant son. Captured, Henrietta, five years old. Escaped: John, Gottlieb and Lizzie Lehn, his stepchildren; Tillie, Caroline, and Minnie, his own children, and Justina his wife. Henrietta was captured and was at Camp Release, and the fate of a baby boy is unknown. Justina was wounded with buckshot, and her clothes stripped from her, but later revived and clothing herself at their home, started for the fort. Wandering about in a dazed condition, she was rescued by Capt. Grant's company, but lay in a wagon during the entire Birch Coulie battle unscathed. In nearly all histories, her thrilling story is found. Later she married John J. Meyer, whose family were all killed at Zitlaff's." See Satterlee, *Account*, 32–33. For a lengthy account of the Krieger family, see Berghold, *The Indians' Revenge*, 162–76.
22. Regarding August Gluth, he was fourteen years old, and surrendered at Camp Release. See Satterlee, *Account*, 91.
23. Battle of Wood Lake took place, September 23, 1862. See note 39 for a description of this particular battle.
24. Regarding Gustaf Kitzmann, see note 5.

25. Regarding Mrs. Lammers and Mrs. Frass, both were from the Middle Creek settlement. William Lammers and August Frass were both killed at their farms, and their wives and families were captured, and surrendered at Camp Release. See Satterlee, *Account*, 33–34, 91–92.
26. Regarding Mrs. Eisenreich and her children, the Balthasar Eisenreich family lived near the mouth of Beaver Creek. The family, together with others, had started off for the fort when her husband was killed. She and the children were captured and surrendered at Camp Release. See Satterlee, *Account*, 25–26, 91.
27. Regarding Kraus and Henrietta Nichols, the Krause family lived at Sacred Heart, and were surrendered at Camp Release. Nichols was twelve years old, and also surrendered at Camp Release. See Satterlee, *Account*, 92.
28. Satterlee reports no other information available on the Nichols family, although the daughter was found at Camp Release. See note 27.
29. "Schmidt, Minnie, four year, at Middle Creek, died at Fort Ridgely in a few days." See Satterlee, *Account*, 93.
30. Schwandt was also at the time more fluent in the English language.
31. This comment indicates the problem in ever establishing a complete list of those killed, as many corpses would not be found.
32. Custer's Seventh Cavalry was said to have included German Americans. See Frederick Whittaker, *Custer: Frederick Whittaker's Complete Life of General George A. Custer, Major General of Volunteers, Brevet Major U.S. Army and Lieutenant Colonel, Seventh U.S. Cavalry*, ed. Don Heinrich Tolzmann (Bowie, Maryland: Heritage Books, Inc., 1993), esp. 1:337–48, which deals with the Seventh Cavalry.

## Chapter 3, Other Related Reminiscences

1. Regarding Godfrey, see note 6 to the preceding Schwandt account.
2. Satterlee notes that Godfrey was also accused of bragging of murders, but of seven, rather than seventeen. See Satterlee, *The Court Proceedings*, 6.
3. Regarding the incident of a baby having been tossed into an oven, see Berghold, *The Indians' Revenge*, 178, where he reports that: "the Indians found another woman baking bread. They took her baby and cast it into the oven, and compelled the bewildered woman to roast it; and then took the roasted flesh and threw it in her face. They finally mutilated the woman in a most horrible manner."
4. Regarding Eusebius Reyff: A resident at Middle Creek, he "was getting up hay, and was in his barnyard with a load, when he and his son Benjamin were killed. The wife and daughter Annie were killed in the door yard. A daughter Mary, and son Emanuel were absent at the time." See Satterlee, *Account*, 29.
5. Regarding Frederic Krieger, see note 21.
6. "Emil Grundmann, wife, and two children were killed. One little daughter had one hand shot off, and was with a younger brother, two children of Horning,

two of Thiel (or Tille), two of Krieger, Mrs. Anna Zabel, left for dead but later revived. These and some others who had escaped to the woods gathered at the Krieger house, but later, becoming alarmed some ran into the woods, leaving the younger and badly wounded children behind. Indians came and burned the house, and with it, either dead or alive, seven children." See Satterlee, *Account*, 33.

7. The Battle of Birch Coulee took place September 2, 1862. See A. P. Connolly, *Minneapolis and the G.A.R.: With a Vivid Account of the Battle of Birch Coulee, Sept. 2 and 3., the Battle of Wood Lake, Sept. 23, the Release of the Women and Children Captives at Camp Release, Sept. 26, 1862*. (Minneapolis, Minnesota: A.P. Connolly, 1906) and J. R. Landy., James Joseph Egan, and Robert Knowles Boyd, *The Battle of Birch Cooley as described by two of the participants, J. J. Egan and Robert Boyd*. (Olivia, Minnesota: Olivia Times, 1926). The latter is a monograph commemorating the "64th Anniversary, September 2, 1926." and can be located at the Minnesota Historical Society.
8. Regarding Mrs. Zabel, see note 6.
9. Regarding John Meyer, see note 12.
10. Regarding Mrs. Sieg, see note 12.
11. Regarding Mr. Hauf, in the Middle Creek settlement, Hauf was with the family of Zitlaff and others, mentioned in note 12, and the group "had driven only a few rods, when the Indians rose from a corn-field and attacked them, killing all but Thiele, Meyer, Mrs. Inefeldt and child and Mrs. Michael Zitlaff. The men escaped in the underbrush. A few minutes later Mrs. Zitlaff was shot and killed. Hauf, taking a child under each arm, started to run, but was shot down and his girls kicked to death, ending his family. Zitlaff is usually given as Sitzton in the meagre and incomplete accounts." See Satterlee, *Account*, 27.
12. Regarding Minnie Krieger, see note 21.

**Editor's Conclusion**

1. Regarding the Civil War, see Thomas L. Livermore, *Numbers and Losses in the Civil War in America, 1861–65* (Rept., 1900 ed.; Carlisle, Pa.: John Kallmann, 1996) and Frederick Phisterer, *Statistical Record of the Armies of the United States: Campaigns of the Civil War, Supplementary Volume*. (Rept., 1883 ed.; Carlisle, Pa.: John Kallmann, 1996).
2. Oehler, *The Great Sioux Uprising*, 143.
3. Ibid., 144.
4. Ibid.
5. Wayne E. Webb, *Redwood the Story of a County* (Redwood Falls, Minnesota: Redwood County Board of Commissioners), 116.
6. Curtiss-Wedge, *Renville County*, 2:1342. For a list of the various monuments and markers found in Brown County, see Elroy E. Ubl, *New Ulm Area Defend-*

ers of August, 1862: Dakota Indians and Pioneer Settlers. (New Ulm, Minnesota: Local History, 1992), 43–49.
7. Ibid., 1346.

# Sources

[*Note: Works of general interest are listed here as a guide to the basic sources, as bibliographical references to sources cited can be found in the footnotes throughout this work.*]

For a comprehensive history of Minnesota, see William Watts Folwell, *A History of Minnesota*, rev. ed., 4 vols. (St. Paul: Minnesota Historical Society, 1956–69), and for a more recent survey, see Theodore C. Blegen, *Minnesota: A History of the State, With a New Concluding Chapter, A State that Works, by Russell W. Fridley* (Minneapolis: University of Minnesota Press, 1975).

Especially useful for this work are the county histories for Renville, Brown, and Redwood Counties: Franklyn Curtiss-Wedge, ed., *The History of Renville County, Minnesota*, 2 vols. (Chicago: H. C. Cooper Jr., & Co., 1916); *Renville County History Book 1980* (Dallas, Texas: Taylor Publishing Co., 1981); L. A. Fritsche, *Brown County (New Ulm) Minnesota Pioneers and Their Families. Excerpted from History of Brown County, Minnesota: Its People, Industries and Institutions*, ed with a new introduction by Don Heinrich Tolzmann. (Baltimore, Maryland: Clearfield Co., Inc., 2001); Wayne E. Webb and Jasper Swedberg, *Redwood, the Story of a County* (Redwood Falls, Minnesota: Redwood County Board of Commissioners, 1964).

Regarding the uprising, see Minnesota Board of Commissioners on Publication of History of Minnesota in Civil and Indian Wars, *Minnesota in the Civil and Indian Wars, 1861–65*, 2d ed. (St. Paul: The Board, 1891); C. M. Oehler, *The Great Sioux Uprising* (New York: Oxford University Press, 1959); Kenneth Carley, *The Sioux Uprising of 1862*, 2d ed. (St. Paul: Minnesota Historical Society, 1976); and *The War for the Plains*. (Alexandria, Virginia: Time Life, Inc., 1994).

An essential fact book on the topic is Marion P. Satterlee, *Outbreak and Massacre by the Dakota Indians in Minnesota in 1862: Marion P. Satterlee's Minute Account of the Outbreak, with Exact Locations, Names of All Victims, Prisoners at Camp Release, Refugees at Fort Ridgely, etc. Complete List of Indians Killed in Battle and Those Hung, and Those Pardoned at Rock Island, Iowa*, ed. Don Heinrich Tolzmann (Bowie, Maryland: Heritage Books, Inc., 2001). Regarding the defense of New Ulm, see Russell W. Fridley, *Charles E. Flandrau and the Defense of New*

*Ulm,* eds. Russell W. Fridley, Leota M. Kellet and June D. Holmquist (New Ulm: Brown County Historical Society, 1962).

For works recording the German-American experience of 1862, see Alexander Berghold, *The Indian's Revenge, or, Days of Horror: Some Appalling Events in the History of the Sioux* (San Francisco, California: P. J. Thomas, 1891), which also appeared in German as, *Indianer-Rache, oder die Schreckenstage von Neu-Ulm* (Graz: Verlags-Buchhandlung Styria, 1892); Jacob Nix, *The Sioux Uprising in Minnesota, 1862: Jacob Nix's Eyewitness History: German/English Edition,* ed. by Don Heinrich Tolzmann (Indiana: Max Kade German-American Center & Indiana German Heritage Society, 1994); and L. A. Fritsche, *Memories of the Battle of New Ulm: Personal Accounts of the Sioux Uprising: L. A. Fritsche's History of Brown County, Minnesota (1916),* ed. Don Heinrich Tolzmann (Bowie, Maryland: Heritage Books, Inc., 2001).

For a survey of the Minnesota Germans, see the essay by Hildegard Binder Johnson in June Drenning Holmquist, ed., *They Chose Minnesota: A Survey of the State's Ethnic Groups* (St. Paul: Minnesota Historical Society, 1981), and for more comprehensive coverage, see Clarence A. Glasrud, ed., *German-Americans in Minnesota: A Collection of Three Volumes* (Moorhead, Minnesota: International Language Villages, Concordia College, 1985).

The best bibliography on the Minnesota Germans is LaVern J. Rippley, "Bibliography for Teaching About Minnesota Germans," in: Paul A. Schons and Thomas E. Klein, *Minnesota AATG Resources Directory 1991* (St. Paul, Minnesota: Minnesota Chapter of the American Association of Teachers of German, 1991), 96–118. More recent references about the Minnesota Germans can be found in LaVern J. Rippley and Robert J. Paulson, *The German-Bohemians: The Quiet Immigrants* (Northfield, Minnesota: St. Olaf College Press, 1995).

# Index

In order to facilitate further research, authors and publications cited are included within this index. The names of authors are printed in small capitals and the names of publications are printed in either italics for general publications or quotations for articles within those publications.

## A
Acton, Minnesota, 5–6
Adams
    Hattie, 53
    Mrs., 21, 51
Agency massacre, 6
Agent Galbraith, 5
ANDERSON, GARY CLAYTON, 80–82
Anderson, Mary, 11–13, 15–17
Attack at New Ulm (engraving), 14

## B
BAKEMAN, MARY HAWKER, 82
*Basic Rules of the Geneva Conventions and Their Additional Protocols*, 83
Battle of Birch Cooley, 69
*Battle of Birch Cooley, The* (Landy, Egan, Boyd), 92
Battles
    Acton, 7
    Birch Cooley/Coulee/Coulie, 6–7, 69, 90, 92
    Forest City, 7
    Hutchinson, 7
    New Ulm, ix
    Wood Lake, 6–7, 20, 72, 83, 85
Beaver Creek, settlements, 12
Beaver Falls, Minnesota, 9
BERGHOLD, ALEXANDER, 86, 90–91, 96
Berghold, Rev. Alexander, 86
"Bibliography for Teaching About Minnesota Germans," *Minnesota AATG Resources Directory 1991* (Rippley), 96
Big Eagle, 6
Big Stone Lake, 2
    attack, 7
Big Woods settlements, 6
BLEGEN, THEODORE C., 95
Boelter
    baby, 36
    Emilia, 90
    Gottlieb, 89
    Grandma, 36
    house of, 35
    John, 89
    Julius, 89
    Justina, 36, 89
    Justine, 90
    Michael, 36, 89–90
    Mr., 34
    Mrs. Justina, 36
    Mrs., 36
BOYD, ROBERT KNOWLES, 92
Brandenburg, District of, 9
Brill, Rev., 30
BRISBOIS, LOUIS G., 88
*Brown County (New Ulm), Minnesota Pioneers and Their Families. Excerpted from History of Brown County, Minnesota, Its People, Industries and Institutions. With an Introduction by Don Heinrich Tolzmann* (Fritsche), 88, 95
Brown County Historical Society, xiii
Brown County, Minnesota, 1–2
BRYANT, CHARLES S., 83–84
Buce/Buse/Busse
    Amelia, 29, 33–35, 50, 58
    August, 29, 32–35, 37
    Augusta, 29, 33, 35, 58
    Bertha, 33, 43
    Caroline, 29, 33–34
    Charley 35

Fred, 52
Gottfried, 29
Minnie, 52
Mr., 64
place of, 64
Wilhelmina ("Minnie"), 79
Wilhelmina, ix–x, 27, 29
Bucholtz
family, 69
Bushe, house of, 86

**C**
Camp Release, 7, 21, 36
Camp Release, (engraving), 21
Campbell, Joseph, 17
Canada, escape to, 86
*Captured by the Indians* (Carrigan), 79
CARLEY, KENNETH, 79, 82, 95
Carrigan
Minnie Bruce 61
Mrs. Minnie Buce, 27, 62
Owen, 58
Wilhelmina ("Minnie") 79
Wilhelmina Buce (photo), 26
CARRIGAN, MINNIE BUCE, 79
*Charles E. Flandrau and the Defense of New Ulm* (Fridley), 95
Chaska, 85
Chaskadon, 85
Chippewas, 5, 65
church society
Middle Creek division, 31
Sacred Heart division, 31
Civil War, 28
claims commission, 22
Congressional Act
Dakota lands in Minnesota, 4
CONNOLLY, A. P., 92
Council, 5
*Court Proceedings in the Trial of Dakota Indians Following the Massacre in Minnesota in August 1862, The* (Satterlee), 81, 91
Courthouse of the Military Commission, The (engraving), 5
Crow Creek reservation, 6
CURTISS-WEDGE, FRANKLYN, xiii, 80–81, 87–88, 92, 95
*Custer, Frederick Whittaker's Complete Life of General George A. Custer, Major General of Volunteers, Brevet Major U.S. Army and Lieutenant Colonel, Seventh U.S. Cavalry* (Whittaker), 91
Custer, Gen., 58
Custer's Seventh Cavalry, 91

Cut Nose, 89

**D**
Dakota
reservation, 86
Territory, escape to, 86
Dakota Conflict/War, 1
Dakota Indian warriors, 1
Dakota Territory
Crow Creek, 7
escape to, 82
David, Le Grand, 10
Davis, Mr., 11–12, 15
De Camp, Mrs., 16
death toll estimates by
Galbraith, Thomas, 81
President Lincoln, 81
*St. Peter Tribune*, 80
Swisshelm, Jane Grey, 80
Donnelly, Ignatius (Minn. Lieut. Gov.), 81

**E**
EGAN, JAMES JOSEPH, 92
Eisenreich
Balthasar, 91
Mrs. and children, 91
Mrs., 49
Elysian, Minnesota, x
Emde
Mr. and Mrs., 57
Mr., 57
Mrs., 57
Rev. Friedrich, 57–58

**F**
Fairwater, Wisconsin, 22
Faribo
John, 61
Oliver, 61
First Battle of New Ulm, 7
Flandrau, Charles E., 7
FLANDRAU, CHARLES E., 81
Flora Township, Minnesota, 78
FOLWELL, WILLIAM WATTS, xiii, 81, 95
Forest City, Minnesota, 62
Fort Ridgely
attack, 6
first attack, 7
location, 13
major attack against, 7
military post, 2
Fort Snelling, 7
Fox Lake, Wisconsin, 29
Fraktur, x
Frass

86
August, 64, 91
John, 76
Mr., home of, 70
Mrs., 49, 91
FRIDLEY, RUSSELL W., 95–96
FRITSCHE, LOUIS A., 81, 88, 95–96
Fross, John, 9

G
Galbraith
  Agent, 5
  Thomas (Indian agent), 81
  Thomas J., 82
*Garland Library of Narratives of North American Indian Captivities,* 79
Gebhard, Darla, xiii
Geneva Conventions, 75, 82
German
  immigrants, 1
  immigration
    great wave of, 83
  settlements, 3
German Lake settlement, xi
*German-American Experience, The* (Tolzmann), 83
*German-Americans in Minnesota* (Glasrud, ed.) 96
*German-Bohemians, The* (Paulson), 96
*Germans in the American Civil War, With a Biographical Directory, The* (Kaufmann), 87
Germany, Berlin, 9
GLASRUD, CLARENCE A., 96
Gleason, George, 85
Gluth, August, 49, 55, 90
Godfrey
  91
  Joe, 61
  Joseph, 7, 83–84
Good Thunder (also Wakin-yan Weste), 18–19
Good Thunder, 6, 84
*Great Sioux Uprising, The* (Oehler), 81, 86–87, 92, 95
Grundmann
  Emil, 64, 91
  wife and two children, 91
Guess, August, 66, 68, 74

H
Hauf
  Ernest, 89
  Mr., 71, 92

Helenville, Jefferson County, Wisconsin, 62
Henderson
  horses of Mr., 70
  team of, 89
Henrietta, 41
*History of Brown County, Minnesota* (Fritsche), 81
*History of Minnesota, A* (Folwell), 81, 95
*History of Redwood County, Minnesota, The* (Curtiss-Wedge), 81
*History of Renville County, Minnesota, The* (Curtiss-Wedge), 80, 95
*History of the Great Massacre by the Sioux Indians in Minnesota, Including the Personal Narratives of Many Who Escaped, A* (Bryant), 83–84
*History of the Spirit Lake Massacre! 8th March, 1857, and of Miss Abigail Gardner's Three Month's Captivity Among the Indians. According to Her Own Account, As Given to L. P. Lee* (Lee), 82
HOLMQUIST, JUNE DRENNING, 96
HOMSTAD, DANIEL W., 82
Honey Creek (or Sacred Heart), 9
Horning, children of, 91
Huggan, Mrs., 17
Hunter, Mrs., 18
Hutchinson, Minnesota, 6, 57

I
*Indian Agents of the Old Frontier* (Seymour), 81–82
Indian Bureau, 4
Indian Camp at Redwood (engraving) 3
Indian tribes
  Chippewas, 28, 65
  Sioux, 28
  Wapekuta, 84
Indian village
  Shakopee, 10
Indian villages, location of, 2
*Indian's Revenge, or, Days of Horror, The* (Berghold), 86, 90, 96
*Indianer-Rache, oder die Schreckenstage von Neu-Ulm* (Berghold), 96
Infeld/Inefeldt
  Mrs. Minnie, 51
  Mrs., 32, 42, 49, 57, 61, 70, 89, 92
  William, 89
Inkpaduta (Scarlet Point), 81
Inkpaduta affair, 6
Inkpaduta, 82

Iowa
  Lake Okoboji, 81
  Rock Island, 84
Isolated Cloud, (Marpia-wita), 5

**J**
Jackson County, Minnesota, 81
Jefferson County, Wisconsin, 62
JOHNSON, HILDEGARD BINDER, 96
Juni
  Ben, 51
  Lena, 70, 89
  Mary (Mrs. John Zitlaff), 89
  Mary, 32

**K**
KALLMANN, JOHN, 92
KAUFMANN, WILHELM, 87
KELLET, LEOTA M., 96
*Kinsmen of Another Kind* (Anderson), 82
Kitzman/Kitzmann
  87
  family 29
  Gustaf, 48, 88, 90
  John, 69
  Louis, 64, 88
  Ludwig, 43, 45, 49, 51, 54, 57, 90
  Mike, 69
  Minnie, 58
  Mr., 29
  Paul (infant), 88
  Paul, 64–65, 88, 90
  Pauline, 58, 88
  wife of Paul, 88
  Wilhelmina, 88
KLEIN, THOMAS E., 96
Kochendurfer/Kochendorfer
  87
  John, 90
  Mrs., 38
  place of, 63
  Sarah, 90
Kraus/Krause/Krus
  87
  family, 91
  Mr., 65–66
  Mrs., 49–50, 52, 54, 56
  Pauline, 49
  place of, 65–66
Krieger
  Caroline, 72
  children of, 92
  Frederic/Frederick/Friedrich, 64, 90–91
  Gottlieb, 68, 74
  Henrietta, 44, 51, 57, 69, 90
  John, 68
  Lizzie, 72–73

Minnie, 70, 72, 92
Mr., 65
Mrs., 69–70
Tillie, 72

**L**
La Blaugh, Antoine, 12
La Crosse, Wisconsin, 68
Lake Shetek, first attack, 7
Lammers
  Mrs., 55, 91
  William, 91
Landmeier
  unknown (hired man), 12
  William, 11
LANDY, J.R., 92
Lane
  Daniel, 64
  John G., 64, 69, 72, 74
  Minnie, 64
Lang
  Mr., 56
  Mrs., 49
Laur, Bill, 62
Le Sueur, Minnesota, 69
LEE, L. P., 82
*Legends, Letters, and Lies* (Bakeman), 82
Lentz/Lenz
  Augusta, 36, 42, 49, 88–89
  Ernest, 88–90
  family, 10, 29
  Mr., 29, 31–32, 36
Lettou
  John, 89
  Mr., 32
Lincoln, President, 81
"Lincoln's Agonizing Decision" *American History* (Homstad), 82
Lincoln's decision, 82
Little Crow
  xiii, 6, 82, 85
  scalp of, 18
  village of, 6, 16, 19
  withdraws, 7
*Little Crow, Spokesman for the Sioux,* (Anderson), 82
LIVERMORE, THOMAS L., 92
Lower Agency
  7, 70
  location of, 12
Lower Indians, 6
Lower Sioux, renegade, 81

**M**
Maggie (see Snana), 18–20
Mankato, 7, 15, 63

Mannweiler
  Gottlieb, 89
  Mr., 29, 32, 36, 64
  Mrs., 36
  place of 64
Marpia-wita, (Isolated Cloud), 5
Marsh, Captain John, 6
Marshall, Col. Wm. R., 83
Mary
  (sister-in-law to Mrs. Infield), 71–72
Max Kade German-American Center, ix
*Memories of the Battle of New Ulm*
  (Tolzmann, ed.), 96
Meyer
  92
  John J., 89–90
  John, 70, 92
  Mr., 69, 71–73
  Mrs., 71
Middle Creek Church monument, 79
Middle Creek settlement, 92
Middle Creek, Minnesota, 62
Milford, Minnesota, 78
military commission
  appointment by Sibley, 7
Miller, Mrs., 56, 68
*Minneapolis and the G.A.R., With a Vivid Account of the Battle of Birch Coulee, Sept. 2 and 3., the Battle of Wood Lake, Sept. 23, the Release of the Women and Children Captives at Camp Release, Sept. 26, 1862* (Connolly), 92
Minnesota
  Acton 5
    battle at 7
    murder, 6
  Beaver Falls Township, 2
  Beaver Falls, 9
  Brown County, 1–2
  Brown County, history of, 2
  Cannon Falls, 29
  Elysian, x
  Emmet Township, 2
  Flora Township 78
  Flora Township, 2
  Forest City, 62
  Henryville Township, 2
  Hutchinson, 6, 57
  Jackson County, 81
  Le Sueur, 69
  Meeker County murder, 6
  Middle Creek, 62
  Milford 78
  New Ulm
    x, 13, 33, 83
    attack, 6
    first battle, 7

  population 2
  second battle, 7
  population in 1862, 2
  Redwood County, 1–2
  Renville County
    1–2
    casualties 76
    Flora Township location, 79
    history, 2
    Middle Creek, 29
  Renville County, 28
  Rochester, 69
  Sacred Heart (origin of name) 88
  Sacred Heart Creek
    first settler, 29
  Sacred Heart Township, 2
  St. Paul, 57
  St. Peter, 21–22, 57
  St. Peter, arrival of General Sibley, 7
  Yellow Medicine County, 29, 33
*Minnesota AATG Resources Directory 1991* (Schons & Klein), 96
MINNESOTA BOARD OF COMMISSIONERS ON PUBLICATION OF HISTORY OF MINNESOTA IN CIVIL AND INDIAN WARS, 81, 95
*Minnesota Historical Society Collections* (Schwandt-Schmidt), 79
*Minnesota Historical Society Collections*, ix
*Minnesota History* (Anderson), 82
*Minnesota in the Civil and Indian Wars* (Flandrau), 81
*Minnesota in the Civil and Indian Wars* (Minn. Bd. of Comm.), 81, 95
Minnesota River valley, 6
Minnesota River, 1–2, 30
Minnesota valley, 3, 27
*Minnesota, A History of the State, With a New Concluding Chapter, A State that Works, by Russell W. Fridley* (Blegen), 95
Montana, 58
Mooer
  52
  John, 12
  Mr., 13
Muhs
  John, 57
  Mr. and Mrs., 57
  Mr., 57
Muller
  Dr., 50
  Mrs. Elizabeth, 50
Myrick, Andrew (trader), 5, 82
"Myrick's Insult

A Fresh Look at Myth and Reality,"
*Minnesota History* (Anderson), 82

**N**
Nairn, Mr., 13
"Narration of A Friendly Sioux,"
*Minnesota Historical Society Collections* (Snana), 85
Nebraska
  Santee Agency, 15
Negro
  Godfrey, 15–16
*New Ulm Area Defenders of August, 1862 Dakota Indians and Pioneer Settlers* (Ubl), 92
New Ulm, Minnesota, x, 2, 13, 33, 83
Newspapers
  *Pioneer Press,* 16
  St. Peter *Tribune,* 80
  *The Buffalo Lake News,* 27
Nichols
  Henrietta, 49
Nichols, Henrietta, 49, 91
Nix, Captain Jacob, ix, 7
NIX, JACOB, 79, 96
North Dakota
  Grand Forks County, 69
north ten-mile strip 2
*Numbers and Losses in the Civil War in America, 1861–65* (Livermore), 92

**O**
O, Morgenroth! O, Morgenroth!, 12
O'Connor, Ed., 88
OEHLER, C. M., 80–81, 86–87, 92, 95
Ohio, Painesville, 11
Oregon, Portland, 22
*Outbreak and Massacre by the Dakota Indians in Minnesota in 1862* (Satterlee), 80, 84–86, 88–92, 95
*Over the Earth I Come* (Schultz), 82, 84, 87

**P**
Painesville, Ohio, 11
Patoile, Mr., 12–13, 15
Patterson, Charles, 88
PAULSON, ROBERT J., 96
payment of 1862, 5
PHISTERER, FREDERICK, 92
Portland, Oregon, 22
Prairie on Fire (engraving), 14

**R**
Red Legs, 6
Redwood County, Minnesota, 1–2
Redwood ferry, 6
*Redwood, the Story of a County* (Webb & Swedberg), 81, 92, 95
Reichmann, Eberhard, ix–x
*Renville County* (Curtiss-Wedge), 80–81, 87–88, 92
*Renville County History Book 1980,* 80, 95
Renville County, Minnesota, 1–3, 28
Reyff
  Annie, 64, 91
  Ben, 62
  Benjamin, 91
  Emanuel, 62, 91
  Emma, 63
  Eusebius, 62–63, 91
  family of 64
  Mary, 56, 63, 91
  wife of Eusebius, 91
Reynolds
  family, 10
  J. B., 10
  Mr. and Mrs., 12–13, 15
  Mr., 11, 13, 22
  Mrs. Valencia, 11
  Mrs., 10, 17, 58
Rieke, Mr., 55
Ripon, Wisconsin, 9
RIPPLEY, LAVERN J., 96
Robinson, Mr., 70
Rochester, Minnesota, 69
Rock Island
  83
  prisoners, 6
Roessler
  Frederick, 89
  house of, 33
  John, 89
  Mrs., 33
ROWAN, STEVEN (TRANSLATOR), 87

**S**
Sacred Hat, 88
Sacred Heart (or Honey Creek), 9
Sacred Heart, Minnesota, 88
SATTERLEE, MARION P., 4, 80–81, 83–84, 86, 88–92, 95
Satterlee's Summary, 4
SCHLUTZ, DUANE, 82, 84, 87
Schmidt
  Minnie, 49–50, 56, 91
  Mr. 29
  Mrs., 29, 38, 63

*Index* / 103

place of, 63
William, 22
SCHONS, PAUL A., 96
Schwandt
  August (photo), 23
  August, 9, 11, 21–22, 86
  Christian, 9, 76
  Christina, 9, 76
  family's arrival 88
  Frederick, 9, 76
  home of, 65
  Johann, 76
  John, 9
  Karolina (Mrs. Walz/Waltz), 9, 76
  Mary (photo), 8
  Mary, x, xiii, 9, 42, 49, 51, 53, 83–86
  Memorial, 79
  Mr. 31
  Mrs., 86
Schwandt-Schmidt, Mary, 24
SCHWANDT-SCHMIDT, MARY, 79, 88
Second Battle of Bull Run, 75
Second Battle of New Ulm, 7
Seder, Rev. Mr., 33, 79, 89
September 11, 2001, 1
Seymour, Flora Warren, 81
Shakopee
  61
  camp of, 85
  village of, 83
Sibley
  General, 7, 22
  H. H., 7
Sieg
  John, 89
  Mr., 71
  Mrs., 71, 92
Sioux
  detention camp, 7
  execution, 7
  land 2
  leaders withdraw, 7
  Lower Agency, move to detention camp, 7
  release captives, 7
  surrender, 7
*Sioux Uprising in Minnesota, 1862, Jacob Nix's Eyewitness History, The* (Tolzmann), 84
*Sioux Uprising in Minnesota, 1862, The* (Nix), 79–80, 96
*Sioux Uprising of 1862, The* (Carley), 79, 81–82, 95
Sissetons, (Upper Indians), 6, 20
Sitzton (see Zitlaff), 92

*Six Weeks in the Sioux Teepees (Little Crow's Camp)* (Wakefield), 86
Snahnah, 76
Snana ("Maggie")
  daughter of Wam-nu-ka-win, 18
Snana, 84–85
Soldiers' Lodge, 5
Sperber, Christian
  family of, 80
Spirit Hat, 88
Spirit Lake massacre, 4
St. Paul, Minnesota, 57
St. Peter, Minnesota, 21–22, 57
*Statistical Record of the Armies of the United States* (Phisterer), 92
SWEDBERG, JASPER, 81, 95
Sweet, Mrs., 16, 18
Swisshelm, Jane Grey, 75

T
*The Court Proceedings* (Satterlee), 83
The flowers that bloom in the wildwood, 59
*The History of Renville County, Minnesota*, xiii
"The Story of Mary Schwandt," *Minnesota Historical Society Collections* (Schwandt-Schmidt), 79
*They Chose Minnesota* (Johnson & Holmquist), 96
Thiel/Thiele/Tille
  89, 92
  children of, 92
  Louis, 32, 80, 89
  Mr. And Mrs., 71
  Mr., 32, 52–53, 69, 72
THOMAS, P. J., 86, 96
*Through Dakota Eyes* (Anderson and Woolworth), 80–81
Tolzmann
  Albert (photo) xii
  Carl and Augusta (photo), xi
  Carl, 80
  farm, x, 80
TOLZMANN, DON HEINRICH, 80, 83–84, 87, 91, 95–96
Tolzmann, Eckhart (as consultant), 87
Treaty of 1851, 4

U
UBL, ELROY E., 92
Union Army 2
Upham, Dr. Warren, 76
Upper Agency, 82

Upper Indians (Sissetons), 6
Upper Sioux Agency, 6
Urban
   August, 69
   Mrs., 42, 49–50, 54, 90
   Pauline, 50–51

W
Wacouta
   16
   chief, 16, 84
Wakefield
   Dr., 86
   Mrs. Dr., 21
   Sarah F., 85
WAKEFIELD, SARAH W., 86
Wakin-yan Weste (also Good Thunder), 18
Waltz/Walz
   John 9
   John, 76
   Karolina (nee Schwandt), 9, 76
   Mrs., 10
Wam-nu-ka, 19
Wam-nu-ka-win (old Indian woman) 18
Wapekuta tribe, 84
*War for the Plains, The* (Carley), 81–82, 95
WEBB, WAYNE E., 81, 92, 95
West Lake, first attack, 7
WHITTAKER, FREDERICK, 91
Wie lange und schwer wird die Zeit, 42
Williams
   Mattie 11
   Mattie, 15–17

   Miss, 12–13
Williamson
   Reverend's mission school, 84
Wisconsin
   22
   Fairwater, 22
   Fox Lake, 29
   Helenville, 62
   Jefferson County, 62
   La Crosse, 68
   Ripon, 9
Wood Lake
   Battle of, 85
Wood Lake, 7
WOOLWORTH, ALAN R., 80–81

Y
Yellow Medicine agency, 12
Yellow Medicine County, Minnesota, 29, 33
Yellow Medicine, 19

Z
Zabel
   Mrs. Anna, 92
   Mrs., 70, 73–74, 92
Zitlaff
   family of, 92
   John, 89
   Mary (nee Juni), 89
   Michael, 89
   Mike, 32, 70
   Mr., 32, 71
   Mrs. Michael, 92

## About the Editor

DON HEINRICH TOLZMANN is the Curator of the German-Americana Collection and Director of the German-American Studies Program at the University of Cincinnati. He is the author and editor of numerous works relating to German-American history and culture, which include several on Minnesota's German heritage.

Dr. Tolzmann is shown standing next to the Cincinnati monument that honors Friedrich Hecker, a leader of the 1848 Revolution in Germany. In Cincinnati, Hecker and other Forty-eighters established the first Turner Society in America. In the 1850s, members from that society helped found the frontier settlement of New Ulm, Minnesota.